my grill

my grill
pete evans

OUTDOOR COOKING AUSTRALIAN STYLE

weldon**owen**

contents

the grill

I am an Aussie bloke and I love to cook outdoors on my grill, just as I think every other male does. We take it as our birthright to "man" the grill whenever the occasion arises. Despite this, it was actually my mom who first taught me the fine art of outdoor grilling when I was growing up. I thank my lucky stars for her tong-wielding ability and the lovely dishes she would create for my friends and I after we got back ravenous from a big surf… and, yes, my mom's steak sandwich is included here in all its glory.

Now, the definition of grill is very difficult to pin down as most countries have different ways of cooking and interpreting what a grill actually is. In Australia we call 'barbecuing' anything we cook outdoors over a direct heat whether it be red-hot coals, a gas flame or a simple campfire. After choosing your heat source, there is an array of cooking surfaces to select from, including hotplates, metal grills, hooded ovens to slow-roast in or even smokers to enhance the flavor. But don't get too hung up on the details – the main thing to remember is to enjoy a great meal with friends and family with little stress and some cold beverages to make the day a perfect one.

I've also picked up a few useful tips during my time grilling which I hope will help you to get the best out of your grill. Firstly, I find it helps to brush the grill or griddle with a thin layer of oil before cooking, then preheating your grill to the desired temperature. To maximize flavor and tenderness, meat should be brought to room temperature before grilling and, once cooked, allowed to rest. But, above all, always clean your grill thoroughly after use so that you're ready to fire it up at any time.

This book came about as a way to add some beautiful, simple dishes to your outdoor grilling repertoire. These recipes have served me well, ever since I threw my first 'shrimp on the barbie'. *My Grill* has been broken into three chapters that really showcase my own lifestyle and approach to the grill.

The first chapter, Getting Away, is probably my favorite type of cooking; on a weekend away with the boys or a family vacation. It was photographed at my little hut in the Snowy Mountains in south-east Australia, some camping grounds, and also on my friend Barry's farm (check out his kebab recipe on p68). This chapter offers good, hearty, rustic food, some of which can be cooked in a camp oven – a cast-iron pot with a lid hung over hot coals. The key is to keep adjusting the temperature – by monitoring the fire – so you have a constant heat. The camp oven dishes in this book are all wet so you have very little chance of stuffing it up.

The Lazy Days chapter encompasses the classic outdoor grill. It's shot at my place overlooking the ocean on Sydney's Bondi Beach. This chapter is all about carefree cooking, not taking up too much time or energy and getting things straight onto platters for guests to enjoy.

Into the Evening caters for a more stylish dinner party or special occasion. The recipes in this chapter are perfect for when you want to wow your friends and family with your culinary expertise but still with a minimum of fuss. I have even included a dozen or so drink recipes to help make your grill one to remember.

The reason I became a chef is as simple as this: I flunked English and as a result, didn't have the marks to go to university. Thank god for small miracles as cooking has been the best thing that ever happened to me, though, if you told either my English teachers or myself that I would one day have a cookbook in print, I know exactly what they would have said (and I don't think I can write it here). I know my writing won't be winning any Pulitzer Prizes, but when I am sitting down to write recipes and the little stories about their origin, or just rambling about something totally random and really enjoying it, I have to pinch myself. However, I am only a small part of what you are holding in your hands, so I would like to thank the other people responsible for creating this book I am so proud of.

A big thank you to all the team at Murdoch Books for letting me put my thoughts and ideas down on paper; Juliet Rogers and Kay Scarlett for having the faith to keep paddling with me against the current, Jane Lawson for putting it all together with the minimum of fuss, Reuben Crossman for his vision and style, Mary-Jayne House for flying me around the country to have chats with interesting people, Sonia Greig for testing my recipes and Daniela Bertollo for making my words sound like I have half an education... I think you may have the hardest job of all!

To the "dynamic duo", photographer Anson Smart and food stylist David Morgan, a truly remarkable team that can turn the ordinary into something amazing... I don't know how you do it, but I'm glad you do give a damn!

For my teams at my restaurants Hugos and The Pantry, thank you for your constant support each and every day. A big thanks to Monica and Jacinta Cannactaci for your help with both the photoshoot and for preparing everything so perfectly and stress-free, thank you also to Massimo Mele, Kris Bailey, Guy Massey, Matt Drummond, Clint Jaeger and Gerard d'Ombrille for looking after my kitchens.

Thanks again to my business partners, Dave Evans, Dave Corsi, Daniel Vaughan, Guy Mainwaring and Daddy'o for allowing me the time and understanding to follow my dream.

Thank you to all the booksellers helping promote my book and getting it into the kitchens of people everywhere and hopefully putting a smile on family's faces.

The team I worked with at *Fresh* have opened my eyes to so many cuisines over the past few years. Not many people can say they cook nearly 800 totally different meals a year, but I can, thanks to the amazing talents of Michelle Lucia, Rob Cowen and Naomi Smith.

A very big thank you to John Pye for all his work on the book, he's one of the most talented chefs I know and not a bad bloke to have a beer with either.

Mark Ward, the king of cocktails, love your work!

And Andrew Dwyer, for generously sharing a recipe from your cookbook *Outback – Recipes and Stories from the Campfire*.

To the readers and cooks who buy my book, thank you for trusting that I can teach a few knockout recipes and even have a few laughs along the way. If you take just one recipe and incorporate it into your cooking repertoire, then I know this book has been worth it.

Thanks especially to my wonderful family: Astrid, Mom, Udo, Leonie, Poldi, Walter.

Finally, I dedicate this book to my little girls, Chilli and Indii, for helping Daddy clean up after each grilling session. I love you!

Cheers, Pete

getting away

I love getting out of town — going camping, heading to the coast, exploring a national park or fishing from a boat. But what stands out for me in all cases is the meals you enjoy with family and friends. These recipes have all been designed for relaxed vacation and outdoor cooking. I've cooked a couple of dishes in a camp oven — aka a Dutch oven. It works like a baking dish but you cook it over coals or suspend it above the camp fire. Easy and delicious. What could be better than a camp fire, amazing produce, good friends and a few drinks to add a little fuel to the fire.

Some of my favorite ingredients would have to be chorizo sausages. These Spanish pork sausages flavored with paprika are a staple in my fridge (mind you, don't eat too many as they do contain quite a bit of fat, but a little bit here and there shouldn't hurt). They are so versatile — I use them in everything from rice and pasta dishes, with seafood, in stews and, my favorite, with eggs for breakfast. This is a simple recipe that can be cooked on the grill with a minimum of fuss and is a great way to start the day — especially on vacation.

eggs with chorizo

SERVES 4

1 red bell pepper
4 tomatoes, halved
1 Spanish-style cured chorizo
    sausage, cut into slices
1 small handful of torn
    fresh Italian parsley
8 eggs
pinch of smoked paprika
1 cup shredded manchego
    cheese
grilled sourdough bread,
    to serve (optional)

Set up the outdoor grill for direct-heat cooking over high heat. Cook the bell pepper on the grill, turning occasionally, for 15–20 minutes or until the skin turns black. Remove from the grill and let cool. Wipe away the skin leaving the flesh. Cut in half, remove the seeds and stem and cut into strips.

Meanwhile, grill the tomatoes for a few minutes until tender, then cut into chunky pieces.

Place the chorizo on the grill and cook until golden on each side. Cut into slices. Combine in a bowl with the bell pepper, tomato, parsley and salt and pepper.

Place the chorizo and bell pepper mixture in a cast-iron skillet. Place on the grill and make some holes in the mixture to crack the eggs into. Add the eggs, then sprinkle with paprika and manchego cheese. Cover and cook for about 5 minutes or until the egg whites are cooked and the yolks are runny. Serve on grilled sourdough bread.

This recipe is very simple: some eggs, bread and maple syrup or honey for the batter, fried on the grill until golden, then slathered with your favorite toppings. This one features honey, ricotta and figs, which is a great combination on its own but team it with golden french toast and you might just be saying luvvly jubbly, as some famous English chef says.

french toast with figs

SERVES 4

Set up the outdoor grill for direct-heat cooking over medium heat. Place a griddle, *plancha* or *piastra* suitable for use on an outdoor grill on the grill to preheat. Beat the eggs with the maple syrup or honey and a pinch of sea salt. Soak each piece of bread in the egg mixture for about 10 seconds so that the bread gets a bit soggy.

Drain off the excess egg from the bread and place onto the lightly greased griddle. Cook for 2–3 minutes until golden on one side, then flip over and cook until golden on the other side. Set aside on a plate.

Cook the figs, cut-side down, on the griddle for 1–2 minutes or until golden, then place on the platter with the french toast. Drizzle with the honey and dust with confectioners' sugar. Serve with ricotta cheese.

6 eggs
2 tablespoons maple syrup or honey
8 slices of bread (whatever type you like)
8 fresh figs, cut or torn in half
¼ cup organic honey, warmed
confectioners' sugar, to dust
8 tablespoons ricotta cheese

This is a recipe I have been using for more than 15 years — I first started making it at my restaurant The Pantry in Brighton, Australia. It is a great take on the classic pancake recipe as we use ricotta, as well as beaten egg whites, in the batter to lighten it up. I have teamed the pancakes with cinnamon bananas as I am a huge fan of grilled bananas, but please feel free to experiment with whatever fruit is in season — fold some blueberries or raspberries into your batter for an indulgent treat.

ricotta pancakes with cinnamon bananas

SERVES 4

½ cup all-purpose flour
2 teaspoons baking powder
pinch of salt
4 eggs, separated
¾ cup milk
1¼ cups ricotta cheese
clarified butter, for frying (see note)
1 tablespoon ground cinnamon
1 tablespoon superfine sugar
4 ladyfinger or other variety
   bananas (just make sure they
   are very ripe)
8 tablespoons maple syrup
cinnamon stick, broken, for
   garnish (optional)
toasted almonds, to serve (optional)

To make the pancakes, sift the flour, baking powder and salt into a bowl.

In a separate bowl mix the yolks and milk. Slowly add this to the dry ingredients, mixing to combine. Break up the ricotta and add to the batter. Whisk the egg whites in a separate bowl until stiff peaks form and fold into the batter until blended.

Set up the outdoor grill for direct-heat cooking over medium heat. Place a griddle, *plancha* or *piastra* suitable for use on an outdoor grill on the grill to preheat. Grease with some clarified butter. Pour in ½ cup of the batter and cook for about 2 minutes until golden. Flip over and reduce the heat to low. Cook until golden on the second side and remove to a plate. Cover to keep warm. Continue with the rest of the batter.

Combine the cinnamon and sugar. Coat the bananas in the cinnamon sugar and cook on the griddle until crisp and golden. Serve with maple syrup, cinnamon stick and toasted almonds, if you like.

NOTE: To clarify butter, melt 1 cup butter in a small saucepan over low heat for 10 minutes. Pour into a heatproof jug, let stand, skim the surface, then pour off the clear butter and reserve, discarding the milk solids.

This is great for breakfast, brunch or even lunch — it's super-tasty and quite impressive. I think zucchini, corn and feta is a terrific combination – you really want those burnt bits on the edges as they add great texture and flavor. These can be made ahead of time and reheated in the oven or on the grill if needed but, of course, fresh is best. As for the gazpacho sauce, well you are really getting two recipes in one with this dish. Not only does it work really well with the fritters but if you make extra, you can serve the gazpacho as a first course for dinner later that evening.

zucchini & corn fritters with goat cheese & gazpacho sauce

SERVES 4

To make the gazpacho sauce, roughly chop the tomatoes, cucumber, garlic, chile, bell pepper and onion. Place into a food processor or blender with the oil and purée until quite smooth. Pass through a sieve for a refined sauce or leave a bit chunky (whatever you prefer). Add the vinegar and salt and pepper to taste. Refrigerate until ready to use. Just before serving, drizzle with a touch of olive oil.

Place the shredded zucchini in a bowl and sprinkle with sea salt. Let sit for 15 minutes. Squeeze the excess liquid out of the zucchini.

Place two-thirds of the corn into a blender and purée. Add some salt and pepper and the garlic, chile (if using), shallot and cilantro, then purée.

Add the flour and process for 1 minute, then add the egg and process for another 30 seconds.

Pour the mixture into a bowl and fold in the remaining corn, the zucchini, parsley, feta, mint and green onions.

Set up the outdoor grill for direct-heat cooking over medium heat. Place a griddle, *plancha* or *piastra* suitable for use on an outdoor grill on the grill to preheat. Place a ring mold onto the griddle and grease with a bit of oil, then add the zucchini fritter mixture and cook on both sides for about 5 minutes until golden, crisp and cooked through. Repeat with the remaining zucchini mixture.

Spoon some gazpacho sauce on each plate, then top with a couple of fritters and a spoonful of goat cheese.

1¾ cups shredded zucchini

1½ cups raw sweet corn kernels

1 garlic clove, finely chopped

1 long red chile, seeded and finely chopped (optional)

1 shallot, chopped

1 tablespoon chopped fresh cilantro leaves

¼–⅓ cup all-purpose flour

1 egg, lightly beaten

3 tablespoons chopped fresh Italian parsley

2¾ ounces feta cheese, crumbled

2 tablespoons chopped fresh mint

2 green onions, chopped

4 tablespoons fresh goat cheese

GAZPACHO SAUCE

1 pound 2 ounces vine-ripened tomatoes

½ small cucumber, halved, seeded

1 garlic clove

1 red Thai chile

1 red bell pepper, halved and seeded

½ red onion, roughly chopped

¼ cup extra-virgin olive oil, plus more for drizzling

1½ tablespoons red wine vinegar

This is a wonderful way to start the day, especially when you are camping out on vacation. I often cook this before I head off for a half-day of trout fishing, as it's hearty but not too "stodgy" so it fills me up without slowing me down. If you are lucky enough to pick your own mushrooms, then there is no better breakfast dish.

mushrooms on toast with ricotta

SERVES 4

½ cup extra-virgin olive oil
4 garlic cloves, thinly sliced
8 large matsutake mushrooms, or any other type of wild mushroom, thickly sliced
⅓ cup canned whole tomatoes, crushed by hand
1 handful of fresh Italian parsley
8 slices of sourdough bread
4 tablespoons ricotta cheese

Set up the outdoor grill for direct-heat cooking over medium–high heat. Place a heavy, nonreactive saucepan on the grill grate to preheat. Add half the olive oil and fry up the garlic until softened, then add the mushrooms and cook, stirring, until golden, about 10 minutes. Add the crushed tomatoes and season with salt and pepper. Slowly cook for 20 minutes until the sauce reduces slightly, then add the parsley.

Lightly brush the bread with some olive oil and then lightly grill until golden and marked on each side.

Place the bread on a plate, spread with ricotta and serve topped with the mushrooms.

There is a top bloke who goes by the name of John Susman — he is a good friend of mine and is one of the world's most knowledgeable men when it comes to seafood. If you ever get the chance to meet him or, better still, have a beer with him, he will talk to you about food from the ocean like no other man can — and for this reason, when he cooks a piece of fish, you sit up and take notice. This recipe is from the Susman family grill — it's an amazing dish and well worth trying at your next outdoor get-together.

Mr Susman recommends cutting the fish on the diagonal and cooking it right through. I don't mind it cooked to medium — I will leave that up to you. Serve with an icy cold lager.

grilled hamachi with hoisin glaze

SERVES 4

To make the glaze, mix together the hoisin, lime juice, honey, garlic, cilantro and some sea salt and pepper.

Mix together the vegetable and sesame oils and brush over the fish fillets. Let marinate for about 30 minutes.

Set up the outdoor grill for direct-heat cooking over high heat and brush with some of the oil marinade. Cook the fish on the hottest part of the grill, searing for about 1–1½ minutes, then turn over and cook for another 1 minute. Remove from the heat and cover the fish with foil to rest for a few minutes.

Drizzle the hoisin glaze over the fish and serve with steamed jasmine rice.

2 tablespoons vegetable oil
2 teaspoons sesame oil
4 x 6-ounce skinless hamachi fillets,
 cut on the diagonal
steamed jasmine rice, to serve

HOISIN GLAZE
4 tablespoons hoisin sauce
juice of 2 limes
1 tablespoon honey
2 garlic cloves, finely chopped
2 tablespoons chopped fresh
 cilantro leaves

You have to love the classics don't you? I mean, that is what I listen to in my car on the way to work or on a road trip. I sing along to The Beatles, The Doors, Blondie, Bowie, Johnny Cash and Elvis. I can't sing to save myself, but that isn't the point. I love singing as it brings back memories and I know all the words. Some dishes are like that as well, classics, so to speak, and this is one of them — a simple fish dish with a lemon and parsley butter sauce. It is probably one of the first things I ate and also one of the first things I cooked with a fresh catch. I still often cook this dish as it brings back fond memories of that catch, I know all the ingredients and it is very hard to mess up the classics... except, of course, if I'm singing along to them.

halibut with lemon & parsley butter

SERVES 4

all-purpose flour, for coating
4 x 6-ounce halibut or other white-fleshed fin fish fillets
vegetable oil, for cooking
½ cup butter
2 tablespoons chopped fresh Italian parsley
juice of 1 lemon
1 handful of watercress
lemon halves, to serve

Set up the outdoor grill for direct-heat cooking over medium heat. Place a griddle, *plancha* or *piastra* suitable for use on an outdoor grill on the grill to preheat. Put the flour in a bowl and season with salt and pepper. Lightly coat the fish in the seasoned flour.

Lightly oil the griddle. Place the fish on the griddle and cook for about 2 minutes on each side. Remove the fish and keep warm.

Add the butter to a saucepan and cook over high heat for a few minutes — it will just start to brown. Immediately add the parsley, allow to cook for a minute or so, then add a squeeze of lemon juice. Allow the butter to foam, then spoon over the fish and serve with watercress and lemon halves.

I had the good fortune last year to go mushroom foraging in a town called Oberon, which is just past the majestic Blue Mountains, west of Sydney. We were collecting matsutake mushrooms in a pine forest. I was amazed at how many there were and that they were free. Talk about a great tourist attraction — forget truffle hunting in Italy (which I think is overrated). The mushrooms we picked were in our pan that afternoon in a variety of dishes including mushroom bruschetta, steak with mushroom sauce and this one: rainbow trout with wild mushrooms. I had just been fishing in the local river and scored two beautiful brown trout (but I have suggested rainbow here as I think it is a better fish to eat).

Before picking any wild mushrooms, please check with the local tourism board to make sure you have the correct information. Many are poisonous and can be fatal.

trout with wild mushrooms, prosciutto & garlic

SERVES 4

Set up the outdoor grill for direct-heat cooking over medium heat. Using half the butter, place a knob of butter inside each trout, then add a thyme sprig and wrap 5 pieces of prosciutto around each fish. Brush each with 1 tablespoon of the oil.

Cook the fish in a hinged fish basket on the grill for about 4 minutes on each side, then remove and keep warm.

Place a large heavy skillet on the grill and heat the remaining oil until smoking hot. Add the mushrooms and cook for 2–3 minutes, then add the garlic and cook for another minute or so. Add the white wine and parsley and reduce the wine by half, then whisk in the remaining butter. Season with salt and pepper and serve with the trout.

½ cup butter
4 whole rainbow trout, cleaned
 and gutted
4 fresh thyme sprigs
20 very thin slices of prosciutto
4 tablespoons olive oil
1¼ pounds wild mushrooms,
 cleaned and sliced
2 garlic cloves, sliced
1 cup dry white wine
1 handful of fresh Italian parsley,
 finely chopped

This recipe was first featured at my newest restaurant, Hugos Manly, on the beautiful Manly Wharf on Sydney Harbor. I think this is the recipe that really defined the restaurant for me and the clientele — it is a no-nonsense dish that lets the fish do the talking with just a little help from a simple dressing of red wine vinegar, paper-thin slices of garlic and fresh parsley leaves. As a good mate of mine called "Squid" said, "Pete, I think that could be the best fish dish I have ever eaten." That is probably the best compliment I have ever received, as he has been eating fish for the past 45 years and he considers himself to be a bit of a critic when it comes to seafood. And he has been back countless times to eat it.

pacific sole with a warm dressing of garlic, parsley & red wine vinegar

SERVES 4

all-purpose flour, for dusting
4 x 14-ounce whole Pacific soles, or other fish such as baby turbot or plaice
½ cup extra-virgin olive oil
4 garlic cloves, very thinly sliced
1 large handful of fresh Italian parsley
3 tablespoons red wine vinegar
lemon wedges, to serve (optional)

Set up the outdoor grill for direct-heat cooking over medium heat. Place a griddle, *plancha* or *piastra* suitable for use on an outdoor grill on the grill to preheat. Scatter a large platter with the flour and season with salt and pepper. Make 6 incisions across the top of the fish on an angle. Lightly dredge the fish in the seasoned flour and shake off any excess.

Grease the griddle with a little of the olive oil. Place the fish, skin side down, on the griddle and cook for 6–8 minutes, until golden and crisp, then turn over, cover and continue to cook for another 4 minutes or until just cooked through.

Heat the remaining oil and garlic in a saucepan until the garlic is just starting to color. Remove from the heat and add the parsley and red wine vinegar (be careful as it may spit) and season with salt and pepper.

Place the fish on a serving plate and spoon the sauce over the top. Serve with lemon wedges, if you like.

I absolutely love charmoula — the beautiful spice mixture and marinade that is a feature of Moroccan cooking. It brings so many types of meat to life in the simplest of ways. Whether it is spread onto a leg of lamb, or thinly coated onto a fillet of snapper or used to marinate shrimp for your next tagine, it is truly wonderful. You can either make a wet charmoula paste or you can buy a dried charmoula spice mix. This recipe uses the wet one but you could quite easily use the dried mixture – simply dust onto the meat. The best way to serve anything marinated or coated in charmoula is with a simple yogurt and mint sauce.

charmoula-rubbed chicken with yogurt & mint sauce

SERVES 4

To make the yogurt and mint sauce, mix together the cilantro, mint, chile, onion, fish sauce, lime juice and yogurt in a bowl. Do not overmix or the yogurt will split and make the sauce too thin.

To make the charmoula marinade, place the cilantro, parsley, garlic, cumin, ground coriander, paprika, chile and lemon juice in a food processor. While the motor is running, drizzle in the oil and process until smooth. Rub 1 cup charmoula marinade over the chickens and leave to marinate for at least 30 minutes or overnight in refrigerator if possible.

Set up the outdoor grill for direct-heat cooking over medium-high heat. Lightly oil the grill grate and place the chickens on the grill. Cook on one side for 5–10 minutes until golden, then flip and cook another 5–10 minutes until golden. Serve with the yogurt and mint sauce and lemon halves.

4 x 1-pound small chickens, poussins or game hens, butterflied and quartered
lemon halves, to serve

YOGURT & MINT SAUCE
1½ tablespoons chopped fresh cilantro leaves
1 tablespoon chopped fresh mint
1 jalapeño chile, seeded, chopped
1 teaspoon finely diced red onion
1 teaspoon Asian fish sauce
1 teaspoon strained lime juice
⅓ cup thick plain yogurt

CHARMOULA MARINADE
1 large handful of fresh cilantro, leaves, stem and root chopped
1 large handful of fresh Italian parsley, chopped
3 garlic cloves, chopped
2 teaspoons ground cumin
2 teaspoons ground coriander
1 teaspoon paprika
1 Thai chile, seeded, chopped
3 tablespoons lemon juice
4 tablespoons olive oil

What a fabulous recipe this is — it was taught to me by a wonderful chef named Massimo Mele. He's worked all over Australia and one of the places he has worked in happens to be one of my favorite restaurants in Australia — Donovans in St Kilda, Melbourne. This is a wonderful restaurant in a gorgeous location and it's where Massimo learnt this dish. All you need is great-quality shrimp, extra-virgin olive oil, some herbs, chile and a bit of lemon and you are in heaven. Thanks to Massimo and Donovans for the great recipe.

shrimp with chile, oregano & olive oil

SERVES 4

Set up the outdoor grill for direct-heat cooking over high heat. Mix the olive oil with the dried and fresh oregano, red pepper flakes, parsley, lemon zest, garlic and some sea salt and cracked black pepper. Brush the shrimp generously with the oil mixture.

Place the shrimp, shell side down, on the grill and cook for 3 minutes, then turn over and cook for another 30 seconds until just opaque. Remove from the grill, brush the remaining oil mixture over the shrimp and serve.

½ cup extra-virgin olive oil

1 tablespoon dried oregano

1 tablespoon chopped fresh oregano leaves

1 tablespoon red pepper flakes

1 tablespoon chopped fresh parsley

finely grated zest of 1 lemon

1 garlic clove, finely chopped

16 jumbo shrimp, shell on, butterflied from underneath

Can I let you in on a secret? This might have to be the best recipe in the book, especially if you love steak, hate spending time in the kitchen preparing food, and you love the simple things in life. Although a good rib eye is one of the most expensive cuts of meat you can buy, it is worth every cent as I think it's the best cut of meat available. Try to buy a 1-pound 2-ounce piece on the bone to share between two people.

Please, please, please make sure you let the meat rest, otherwise when you slice it (and you do want to slice this to share), all the beautiful juices will run out of the meat and you will have wasted your time and money. Serve with some sautéed broccoli or your favorite salad.

chile salt–crusted rib eye with lemon

SERVES 4

2 x 1 pound 2 ounces rib-eye steaks
¾ cup sea salt
2 tablespoons black peppercorns
1 tablespoon red pepper flakes
1 tablespoon chopped
   fresh rosemary
olive oil
2 lemons, halved

Bring the steaks to room temperature. Set up the outdoor grill for direct-heat cooking over high heat.

In a mortar and pestle, pound the salt, pepper, red pepper flakes and rosemary together. Rub the steak with some olive oil and coat in the spice mixture. Cook on the grill for 5 minutes on each side, then remove from the grill and let stand for 15 minutes. Place the meat back onto the grill and cook until done to your liking, about 2 minutes for medium-rare. Let the meat rest for a few minutes before slicing. Serve with lemon halves and drizzle with extra oil.

I visited a mussel farm last year near Jervis Bay on the beautiful south coast of New South Wales. After collecting mussels from the pristine waters, we headed to Paperbark Camp, an eco-lodge in the area, and I got the chance to cook with their head chef Gary Fishwick, who made the best mussel dish I've ever tasted. I asked Gary what he'd call it when he put it on the menu and he said he'd call it mussels gazwah, which is his nickname, because whenever he can't think of a good name for a dish, he just names it after himself. For this dish, you can wrap the mussels in aluminum foil with the sauce and pop them on the grill.

mussels gazwah

SERVES 4

**4 pounds 8 ounces mussels,
   scrubbed and debearded**
**½ cup plus 1 tablespoon dry
   white wine**

COUSCOUS
1 cup instant couscous
4 dried apricots, finely chopped
6 fresh mint leaves, finely chopped
**1 tablespoon thinly sliced preserved
   lemon peel, rinsed**
1 tablespoon dried currants

GREMOLATA
**1 handful each of fresh basil, mint
   and Italian parsley**
⅓ cup roasted macadamia nuts
finely grated zest of 1 lemon
finely grated zest of 1 lime
½ cup extra-virgin olive oil
⅔ cup fresh bread crumbs

SAUCE
½ cup olive oil
1 onion, chopped
2 teaspoons small capers, rinsed
1 Thai chile, seeded and chopped
3 garlic cloves, chopped
6 anchovy fillets, chopped
**½ cup plus 1 tablespoon dry
   white wine**
⅓ cup tomato paste
½ cup fish broth or clam juice
1 can (14 ounces) crushed tomatoes

Set up the outdoor grill for direct-heat cooking over high heat. To make the couscous, toast the couscous in a large saucepan over high heat until golden brown. Add 1 cup boiling water, cover with a lid and remove from the heat. Let stand for 5 minutes, then remove the lid and stir with a fork to break it up. Add the apricots, mint, preserved lemon and currants. Season to taste with salt and pepper.

To make the gremolata, chop the herbs finely. Chop the macadamias. Combine the herbs, macadamias, zests, olive oil and bread crumbs and season with salt and pepper.

To make the sauce, heat the oil in a heavy-bottomed pot over high heat on the stovetop. Add the onion and sauté until softened. Add the capers, chile, garlic and anchovies and continue sautéing until garlic is golden and anchovies have softened. Then add the wine, tomato paste, broth and tomato. Bring to a boil, then reduce the heat and simmer for 30 minutes. Cool slightly, then purée in a food processor.

Preheat a large Dutch oven on the grill. Add the mussels and wine, cover with a lid and steam until they open, about 5–10 minutes. As there is normally a large amount of salt water that comes out of the mussels once opened, drain most of it, leaving about ½ cup. Add the sauce and toss through the mussels. Serve on the couscous and sprinkle with the gremolata. Kick back and enjoy.

This is one of those special occasion dishes — not to be eaten very often because of the fat content of the pork belly but once every so often it will really warm the soul. It's traditionally cooked in a clay pot which is used in a lot of Southeast Asian cookery, but also translates well to the camp oven or a baking dish with a lid. The saving grace is the spinach, eggplant and rice to balance out the richness of the pork and caramel sauce. It means you can eat it a bit more often if you like.

camp oven pork belly with chile caramel

SERVES 4

Set up the outdoor grill for indirect-heat cooking over medium-high heat, leaving half of the fire bed free of coals. Place a large Dutch oven on the hottest part of the grill to preheat. Add the oil, then add the pork in batches and cook until golden brown. Remove and set aside.

Add the sugar and cook, stirring frequently, for 1 minute, or until the sugar dissolves. Add the garlic, ginger, chile and shallots and cook for 2–3 minutes, or until the sauce turns a deep golden caramel color.

Add the pork, fish sauce, white pepper, a little salt and ¾ cup of water and mix well. Bring to a boil, then move the pot to the cool part of the grill. Cover the grill and simmer for 1 hour, or until the meat is tender. Add the eggplant and cook covered for another 30 minutes. Check the sauce occasionally and add extra water if the sauce becomes too thick or is drying out. Stir in the spinach and serve with steamed rice.

1 tablespoon peanut oil

3 pounds 5 ounces pork belly, halved and cut into 1¼-inch thick slices

½ cup firmly packed light brown sugar

4 garlic cloves, thinly sliced

¾-inch piece ginger, peeled and chopped

1–2 small red chiles, finely chopped

3 shallots, thinly sliced

4 tablespoons Asian fish sauce

1 teaspoon ground white pepper

1 pound Japanese eggplant, cut into bite-sized pieces

4 cups spinach leaves

steamed jasmine rice, to serve

One of the nicest blokes I have ever met is Ian "Herbie" Hemphill. Ian has a shop in Sydney called Herbie's Spices and from there he distributes his spices all around the world. My favorite spice mixture is his tagine mix, which is a great blend of paprika, cardamom, chile and allspice, to name a few. Buying quality pre-made spice blends can save you a lot of time and effort. I love this method of cooking lamb shanks. A camp oven gives the dish so much flavor and it's great to make when away on vacation.

camp oven lamb tagine by herbie

SERVES 4

8 small lamb shanks
4 tablespoons tagine mix (see
   recipe below and note)
2 tablespoons vegetable oil
2 parsnips, peeled and cubed
4 carrots, chopped
3 onions, finely chopped
6 pitted prunes
3–4 black peppercorns, crushed
8 garlic cloves, minced
2 tablespoons tomato paste
1 can (14 ounces) crushed tomatoes
2 cups orange juice
freshly cooked couscous, to serve
chopped fresh Italian parsley,
   to serve

TAGINE MIX
2½ tablespoons mild paprika
5 teaspoons ground coriander seeds
2 teaspoons ground cinnamon
2 teaspoons red pepper flakes
1 teaspoon ground allspice
½ teaspoon ground cloves
½ teaspoon green cardamom seeds

Set up the outdoor grill for indirect-heat cooking over medium-high heat, leaving half of the fire bed free of coals. Place a large Dutch oven on the hottest part of the grill to preheat. Coat the shanks with 3 tablespoons of the tagine mix, add oil to the Dutch oven and sear the shanks lightly in batches.

Return all the shanks to the Dutch oven. Add the parsnips, carrots, onions, prunes, remaining tagine mix, peppercorns, garlic, tomato paste, tomatoes, orange juice and 4 cups of water. Cover the pot with a lid or aluminum foil. Move the pot to the cool part of the grill, cover the grill and gently simmer for 1½–2 hours, or until the meat is very tender. Season with salt. Serve with couscous and chopped parsley.

NOTE: This tagine mix makes more than 4 tablespoons. Store extras in an airtight container for up to 1 month. Alternatively, you can buy tagine mix from gourmet food stores or spice purveyors.

This is another terrific camp oven meal that is so delicious, it definitely needs to be tried once in your lifetime. It's based on a Moroccan tagine and the thing I love about it is that is uses rabbit — so succulent. The addition of the pistachios and apricots really rounds out the dish.

camp oven slow-cooked rabbit with cinnamon, dried apricots & pistachios

SERVES 4

Set up the outdoor grill for indirect-heat cooking over medium-high heat, leaving half of the fire bed free of coals. Place a large Dutch oven on the hottest part of the grill to preheat. Add the oil and sauté the rabbit in the Dutch oven until golden brown. Remove the rabbit and add the onion, celery and garlic and cook for another 2–3 minutes or until softened. Add the cumin, coriander and cinnamon and gently cook for another 5 minutes. Return the rabbit to the pot and add the tomatoes, bay leaf, pistachios, dried apricots and chicken broth.

Cover with a lid. Move the pot to the cool part of the grill. Cover the grill and simmer for another 1 hour 15 minutes or until the rabbit is tender. Remove from the heat and season with salt and pepper.

Serve with mashed potatoes or couscous, with chives tossed through.

½ cup olive oil
1 rabbit, cut for stewing (ask your butcher)
1 onion, finely chopped
1 celery rib, finely chopped
2 garlic cloves, crushed
1 tablespoon ground cumin
1 tablespoon ground coriander
3 cinnamon sticks
1 can (28 ounces) crushed tomatoes
1 bay leaf
¾ cup shelled pistachios
1 cup dried apricots
1 cup chicken broth
mashed potatoes or couscous, to serve
chopped fresh chives, to serve

This recipe comes from Andrew Dwyers, a good friend of mine who runs tours in the outback of Australia. In a nutshell, he takes overseas visitors on safari like no other in the world, where you get to see the real Australia, camping in the desert under the stars, being told stories of Australian folklore and eating delicious meals like this one. He is a damn fine cook. It's one of the best ways I have ever eaten lamb and he's generously allowed me to share the recipe here.

camp oven-roasted leg of lamb with port & onions

SERVES 4

**1 bone-in leg of lamb, about
    6 pounds**
5 garlic cloves, sliced
12 anchovy fillets, cut in half
24 small rosemary sprigs
4 onions
3 tablespoons olive oil
2 cups port
¼ cup butter, cut into cubes

Make a ½-inch deep incision in the top of the lamb with the tip of a knife. Stuff the hole with a slice of garlic, half an anchovy and a sprig of rosemary. Repeat this in a criss-cross pattern across the whole top of the lamb at 1-inch intervals until the garlic, anchovies and rosemary are used up.

Set up the outdoor grill for indirect-heat cooking over medium-high heat, leaving half of the fire bed free of coals. Place a large Dutch oven on the hottest part of the grill to preheat.

Peel and halve the onions, place, sliced side down, in the Dutch oven and add the lamb. You may have to break the end of the leg bone to fit it in. Baste with the olive oil and season with salt and pepper. Pour in the port.

Move the pot to the cool part of the grill. Cover the grill and simmer the lamb for 1½ hours, or until cooked to your liking.

Remove the meat to a plate or board, cover with a clean dish cloth and allow to rest while you make the sauce.

Return the Dutch oven to the hottest part of the grill. Remove the onions. Bring the cooking juices to a boil and reduce to a sauce consistency. Whisk in the butter cubes and serve immediately with the sliced lamb.

This is a fantastic way to present a whole side of salmon or trout that will make your next barbecue a standout. With curries, you usually fry off the curry paste, then cook out your coconut milk and spices and this usually takes a bit of time. Not so with this way — you just mix the paste with the coconut milk and other aromatics and spread it over the side of salmon. The curry mixture really gets into the flesh of the salmon, imparting its delicious flavor. Place this on the center of the table with some steamed rice and Asian greens for a very impressive lunch or dinner.

easy grilled curried salmon

SERVES 4

Remove all bones from the salmon using pliers or tweezers, then score the flesh in a criss-cross pattern.

Combine the curry paste, coconut cream, sugar, fish sauce, cilantro root and stem, lemongrass and half the oil and mix well.

Rub the mixture evenly over the salmon and let marinate for at least 20 minutes.

Set up the outdoor grill for direct-heat cooking over medium-high heat. Place a griddle, *plancha* or *piastra* suitable for use on an outdoor grill on the grill to preheat. Grease the griddle with the remaining oil. Place the salmon on the griddle, skin side down. Cover and cook for about 10 minutes, or until the fish is just cooked through. Remove from the heat and cool slightly before serving. Top with fried shallots, kaffir lime strips and cilantro, and serve with lime halves.

NOTE: Coconut cream (thicker than coconut milk) can be found in Asian markets. Do not substitute with sweetened cream of coconut.

Look for fried shallots, kaffir (makrut) lime and other Asian ingredients in Asian markets.

1 side of Altantic salmon, about 1 pound 10 ounces
1 tablespoon Thai red curry paste
½ cup coconut cream (see note)
2 teaspoons light brown sugar
2 tablespoons Asian fish sauce
2 tablespoons finely chopped fresh cilantro root and stem
2 lemongrass stalks (white part only), finely sliced
4 tablespoons olive oil
3 tablespoons store-bought fried shallots
1 kaffir (makrut) lime leaf, finely julienned
½ cup coarsely chopped fresh cilantro, plus extra for garnish (optional)
lime halves, to serve

I know a lot of people say that you shouldn't do too much or add too many strong flavors to a piece of fish. I agreed in principle – until I tried this dish, which changed my mind entirely. Freshly chopped coconut with chiles, cilantro, mint, turmeric and cumin made into a paste and smothered over a freshly caught fish and cooked either in foil or banana leaves really makes you glad that people advanced from just the plain old crumbed versions of fish.

indian-spiced grilled fish in banana leaves

SERVES 4

2 fresh banana leaves, center veins removed
4 x 6-ounce pieces of trout or other white-fleshed fish
lime halves, to serve

COCONUT CHUTNEY
peeled flesh of 1 fresh coconut (about 12 ounces), coarsely chopped (see note)
3 green serrano chiles, coarsely chopped
1 large handful of fresh cilantro leaves
3 large handfuls of fresh mint
½ cup vegetable oil
2 garlic cloves, crushed
½ teaspoon ground turmeric
1 teaspoon cumin seeds
juice of 2 limes
¼ teaspoon sugar

To make the coconut chutney, place the coconut, chiles, cilantro, mint, oil, garlic, turmeric, cumin seeds, lime juice, sugar and some salt in a food processor and process until finely minced.

Slowly pass each banana leaf over a medium-high flame until the leaf turns bright green. Alternatively, place the leaf on a griddle and heat until it turns bright green, remove from heat and allow to cool.

Set up the outdoor grill for direct-heat cooking over medium heat. Place a griddle, *plancha* or *piastra* suitable for use on an outdoor grill on the grill to preheat. Place a fish piece on a banana leaf piece. Spread one-quarter of the coconut chutney over the fish. Wrap the leaf around the fish and tie with kitchen string to secure. Repeat with the remaining ingredients.

Place the fish parcels on the griddle and cook for about 4–8 minutes, or until the fish is cooked through. Serve with lime halves.

NOTE: Choose a coconut that feels heavy with no sign of dampness.

Heating banana leaves makes them malleable and easy to fold. If banana leaves are unavailable, use parchment paper or aluminum foil.

Look for coconut and banana leaves in Latin or Asian markets.

How good is a recipe where the ingredients are basically the same as the vacation drink of choice around an outdoor grill? I don't think anything else needs to be said about this recipe except pack napkins...

rum 'n' coke ribs

SERVES 2

Combine all the marinade ingredients in a bowl, then place the ribs in a nonreactive dish and cover with the marinade. Refrigerate overnight.

Set up the outdoor grill for indirect-heat cooking over medium-low heat, leaving half of the fire bed free of coals. Place the ribs in a heavy roasting pan and place on the cool part of the grill. Cover the grill and cook for 1 hour 15 minutes, basting the ribs every 20 minutes with the marinade. Add more coals to the fire or turn up the burner so the grill is medium hot. Remove the ribs from the pan and place directly on the grill grate. Cook for 5 minutes on each side, or until caramelized and lightly charred.

While the ribs are cooking, place some of the marinade in a saucepan on the grill, bring to a boil and reduce by half to serve as a sauce with the ribs.

NOTE: Have plenty of napkins on hand as you will definitely have sticky fingers. Oh, and remember to have extra rum and coke on hand for the chef.

2 racks of pork ribs

MARINADE
1 cup rum
3 cups cola
1$\frac{1}{3}$ cups tomato ketchup
1–2 dashes of Tabasco sauce
2 garlic cloves, minced
4 tablespoons hoisin sauce

This is a wonderful way to serve ribs at your next barbecue — it has the sweet and sour flavors that work so well with pork. The sweetness comes from the maple syrup and sweet soy sauce and the sourness comes from the Chinese black vinegar. The great thing about this dish is that you can prepare everything the day before and you also get the maximum flavor of the marinade. This marinade also works well with chicken drumsticks or wings.

maple syrup & tamarind–glazed pork ribs

SERVES 4

4½ pounds Chinese-style pork ribs (pork belly cut into rib-size portions)

MARINADE
1 cup maple syrup
1 cup sweet soy sauce (kecap manis, see note)
1 tablespoon tamarind concentrate
4 tablespoons oyster sauce
1¼ cups Chinese black vinegar
2 cinnamon sticks
3 star anise

To make the marinade, combine all the ingredients in a nonreactive bowl. Add the ribs to the bowl and coat with the marinade. Cover and refrigerate overnight.

Set up the outdoor grill for indirect-heat cooking over medium-low heat, leaving half of the fire bed free of coals. Place the ribs in a heavy roasting pan, cover with aluminum foil and place on the cool part of the grill. Cover the grill and cook for 30 minutes. Turn the ribs and brush with the marinade. Cover and cook for another 30 minutes, or until caramelized and lightly charred.

NOTE: Look for sweet soy sauce, tamarind concentrate, oyster sauce and black vinegar in Asian markets.

There are no secrets to this burger recipe — this is simply a burger I like to cook on my grill, and then eat with a cold beer while watching the surf roll in.

pete's burger

SERVES 4

4 slices aged Cheddar cheese
1 onion, cut into thick slices
4 slices of uncooked bacon
butter, for the rolls
4 hamburger buns with sesame
   seeds, halved
tomato ketchup or barbecue sauce,
   to serve
8 slices vine-ripened tomato
8 slices cornichons
8 large arugula leaves

PATTIES
1¾ pounds ground chuck
2 garlic cloves, crushed
pinch of red pepper flakes
2 tablespoons chopped fresh
   Italian parsley
pinch of dried oregano
1 egg
¼ cup finely diced onion
2-4 tablespoons fresh bread crumbs
1 tablespoon Dijon mustard

To make the patties, mix all the ingredients in a large bowl and form into 4 patties.

Set up the outdoor grill for direct-heat cooking over medium-high heat. Place the patties on the grill and cook for 5 minutes, then turn and continue cooking for a couple of minutes until just done. A minute before you finish cooking the patties, lay the cheese slices on the patties and let melt. Remove and set aside to keep warm.

Meanwhile, place a griddle, *plancha* or *piastra* suitable for an outdoor grill on the grill to preheat. Cook the onion on the griddle until golden. Cook the bacon on the griddle to your liking.

Butter the rolls and place, butter side down, on the grill and cook until just golden with a bit of crunch to them. Remove and construct your burger starting with some sauce, the patties with cheese, then the bacon, onion, tomato, cornichons and arugula.

I just love dishes where you cook your piece of fish or meat and then spoon over a magnificent dressing. This one is a preserved lemon dressing with fresh herbs such as mint and parsley teamed with coriander seeds, lemon juice and olive oil — perfect for just about any seafood or chicken you can cook on the grill.

grilled whole fish with preserved lemon dressing

SERVES 4

Cut 3 diagonal slashes on each side of the fish down to the bone. Rub with some olive oil and season with salt and pepper. Place the fish in a hinged grill basket.

Set up the outdoor grill for direct-heat cooking over medium heat. Cook the fish for about 4–5 minutes on each side or until golden and crispy (if it needs more cooking move the fish to a cooler part of the grill and cover the grill for a few minutes to cook through).

Meanwhile, make the dressing. Combine all the ingredients in a bowl. Stir well and check for seasoning, adding a little sugar and salt if necessary.

Place the fish on a serving platter and spoon over half of the dressing. Serve with the remaining dressing on the side.

4 x 10-ounce whole sea bass or other white-fleshed whole fish
olive oil, for cooking

PRESERVED LEMON DRESSING
1 tablespoon thinly sliced preserved lemon peel
2 tablespoons small capers, rinsed
pinch of ground coriander seeds
2 tablespoons slivered fresh mint
2 tablespoons slivered fresh Italian parsley
2 tablespoons lemon juice, to taste
6 tablespoons extra-virgin olive oil
sugar (optional)

I am a huge fan of Asian food. I often take the kids down to Chinatown for a big lunch and love ordering the seafood dishes such as clams with XO sauce, whole steamed fish or scallops with ginger and green onions. These days you can buy XO sauce from an Asian grocer, but you can also make your own. The great thing about a recipe like this is that once you have the sauce, there's hardly any preparation needed and within minutes you can be eating a great meal of clams in the time it would take you to drive into Chinatown. Serve with an icy cold beer.

clams with xo sauce

SERVES 4

3 tablespoons XO sauce (store bought or see recipe below)
1¼ pounds clams
1 tablespoon light soy sauce
2 tablespoons chicken broth
6 green onions, cut into 2-inch lengths

XO SAUCE (OPTIONAL)
9 ounces red serrano chiles, seeded and chopped
1 tablespoon finely chopped fresh ginger
2 garlic cloves, roughly chopped
½ ounce dried shrimp, soaked in hot water for 1 hour, drained (see note)
1 ounce dried fish or scallops, soaked in hot water for 1 hour, drained
1 teaspoon salt
1 teaspoon sugar
4 tablespoons vegetable oil

If you are making your own XO sauce, blend all ingredients in a food processor, then pour into a saucepan and cook gently over very low heat for 15 minutes to enhance the flavors without burning.

Set up the outdoor grill for direct-heat cooking over medium heat. Place the clams, XO sauce, soy sauce and chicken broth into a large piece of heavy-duty aluminum foil that has been doubled over. Seal into a package, allowing space for the clams to open by bringing all the sides together and crimping at the top. Place onto the grill and cook for 8–10 minutes or until the clams open up.

Toss with the green onions and serve.

NOTE: Ask the fishmonger if the clams have been purged of sand before you buy them. If not, put them in the fridge overnight in some salted water. This will help remove any sand or grit that may still be in them.

Dried shrimp and dried fish can be found in Asian markets.

Store leftover XO sauce in an airtight jar with a layer of vegetable oil on top in the fridge for 2 weeks.

Udo, my brother-in-law, created this recipe in Australia's Northern Territory last year on a fishing trip that somehow I wasn't invited along to – hence Udo did the cooking this time. He rang and told me about all the magnificent fish and mudcrabs he caught and about this delicious dish he created.

udo's fish in foil with tamarind, coconut milk & other aromatics

SERVES 4

1 large banana leaf
1 whole barramundi, sea bass or other whole fish, about 4½ pounds
lime halves, to serve

PASTE
2 garlic cloves, chopped
1 large knob of ginger, chopped
3 shallots, chopped
2 red serrano chiles, seeded and chopped
1 lemongrass stalk, white part only, chopped
1 small bunch of fresh cilantro, root and leaves, chopped
1 teaspoon shrimp paste (see note)
1 teaspoon light brown sugar
1 teaspoon Asian fish sauce
1 tablespoon tamarind paste
1 can (15¼ fluid ounces) coconut milk or cream

To make the paste, use a mortar and pestle to pound together the garlic, ginger, shallots, chiles, lemongrass, cilantro and shrimp paste until you have a smooth paste. Put the paste in a bowl and add the sugar, fish sauce, tamarind and coconut milk and mix to combine.

Slowly pass the banana leaf over a medium-high gas flame until the leaf turns bright green. Alternatively, place the leaf on a griddle and heat until it turns bright green. Let the leaf cool.

Score the fish, then place it on the banana leaf. Rub the coconut milk paste over the fish, then turn over and repeat. Wrap the leaf around the fish, then wrap with aluminum foil to secure.

Set up the outdoor grill for direct-heat cooking over medium heat. Place the fish on the grill, cover and cook for about 15 minutes, or until just cooked through, turning over halfway through. Serve with lime halves.

NOTE: Heating banana leaves makes them malleable and easy to fold. If banana leaves are unavailable, use aluminum foil.

Shrimp paste, tamarind paste and coconut products can be found in Asian markets.

A very good friend of mine, Barry Aitchison, lives in the Snowy Mountains, in New South Wales, Australia, and he's very generous with his time and knowledge of all things "high country" – from the history to where and how you catch the best fish, and the best way to cook it. We were shooting some of the photos for this book at Barry's and he cooked us these kebabs for lunch, along with a delicious rustic beer bread called a damper – they're so good, they deserve a place in this book.

barry's mixed kebabs with beer "damper"

SERVES 4

To make the damper, combine the flour, sugar and salt in a bowl. Stir in the beer and butter, then lightly knead the mixture until it comes together, transfer to a clean bowl and cover with a dish cloth and leave for about 1 hour.

Set up the outdoor grill for indirect-heat cooking over high heat, leaving half of the fire bed free of coals. Place a large Dutch oven on the grill, directly over the heat. Grease the pot with olive oil or butter and sprinkle with flour. Cook the flour for a couple of seconds (if it turns brown it's too hot) and move to the cool part of the grill.

Add the damper dough to the pot, cover the grill and cook the damper for 30 minutes (if it sounds hollow when it is tapped, it is cooked). Pour a little melted butter over the top when it is cooked. Set aside.

To make the kebabs, combine the lemon, honey and garlic in a nonreactive bowl, add the lamb and toss to coat or leave to marinate for 30 minutes.

Thread the lamb onto metal skewers alternating with green and red bell peppers, mushrooms, pineapple and tomatoes, then brush with some oil. Cook kebabs on hot part of the grill for about 10 minutes, turning every few minutes, or until cooked to your liking.

juice of 1 lemon
2 tablespoons honey
2 garlic cloves, crushed
1¼ pounds lamb leg, cut into cubes
1 green bell pepper, cut into squares
1 red bell pepper, cut into squares
½ cup button mushrooms
½ pineapple, peeled and diced
1½ cups cherry tomatoes
olive oil, for cooking

BEER DAMPER
3 cups self-rising flour
1 tablespoon superfine sugar
pinch of salt
1½ cups beer
2 tablespoons butter, melted, plus extra melted butter

Tom Kime is a chef who came into the TV studio one day and showed me the art of making pickled carrot and spiced squash and it really blew me away. So I've taken the liberty of using these two great accompaniments and added them to a Turkish lamb sandwich as they fit the bill perfectly. Try these delicious recipes on some toasted bread and see what I am talking about.

the best grilled turkish lamb sandwich

SERVES 4

Set up the outdoor grill for direct-heat cooking over medium heat. Coat the lamb in olive oil and season with salt and pepper. Cook on the grill for about 3 minutes or until brown on one side, then turn over and cook the other side. Let rest for 5 minutes before slicing thinly.

Brush the bread with a touch of olive oil and grill lightly.

Spread the spiced squash over the base of the bread, then top with the yogurt, lamb slices, pickled carrots, mint and arugula. Cover with the bread tops and serve.

NOTE: Turkish bread is a wide, flat, yeasted bread available in specialty bakeries.

2 lamb loins
1 tablespoon olive oil
1 large Turkish bread or ciabatta, cut in half lengthwise (see note)
1 batch spiced squash (recipe opposite)
½ cup plain yogurt
½ cup pickled carrots (recipe opposite)
1 small handful of fresh mint
1 bunch of arugula

spiced squash & pickled carrots

MAKES ABOUT 1½ CUPS EACH

SPICED SQUASH

about 1 pound butternut squash,
  peeled, seeded, and cut into
  ¾-inch cubes
1 teaspoon caraway seeds
1 teaspoon cumin seeds
3 garlic cloves, finely chopped
1 small red serrano chile, seeded
  and chopped
4–6 tablespoons extra-virgin
  olive oil
juice of 1 lemon

PICKLED CARROTS

1 tablespoon olive oil
1 garlic clove, finely chopped
1 small red serrano chile, seeded and
  finely chopped
pinch of cayenne pepper
pinch of ground cumin
pinch of ground coriander
pinch of ground allspice
about 1 pound carrots, shredded
¾ cup sugar
⅔ cup malt vinegar

To make the spiced squash, preheat the oven to 425°F.

Place the squash in a baking pan, cover with aluminum foil and roast for 30 minutes, turning occasionally, or until the squash is tender, then season with salt and pepper. Mash the squash with a fork and set aside.

Dry-toast the caraway and cumin seeds in a small skillet over medium-high heat for a couple of minutes until aromatic. Crush the toasted seeds using a mortar and pestle. Cook the garlic and chile in a touch of oil in a small saucepan over medium heat for 2 minutes and mix to combine. Add the spice mixture, garlic and chile to the squash with the lemon juice. Mix well, then stir in the remaining olive oil.

To make the pickled carrots, heat the oil in a small heavy skillet over medium-high heat for 2–3 minutes. Add the garlic and chile, and fry for a couple of minutes until fragrant. Sprinkle in the spices. Cook for another 1–2 minutes until aromatic. Add the carrots, sugar, vinegar and ½ cup of water, and gently simmer over low heat for 40 minutes to 1 hour, stirring occasionally, or until the excess liquid had been cooked off and the carrot is half cooked. Season with salt and pepper.

This recipe is the result of my quest to find a crumbed dish — like a schnitzel, but not your ordinary schnitzel — for an unpretentious menu. After trying veal, chicken, fish and pork, I thought the pork cutlet was the winner. By adding Parmesan and sage into the crumb mixture, it took it from plain and simple to something with that little bit extra. You can team it with a simple garden salad and lemon wedges, or try this elegant fennel salad.

parmesan & sage crusted pork cutlets with fennel salad

SERVES 4

Mix the bread crumbs with the sage and Parmesan. Season the flour with salt and pepper, then lightly dust the pork in the flour and shake off any excess. Dip into the beaten eggs and drain off any excess, then place into the bread-crumb mixture and press down firmly to coat the cutlets evenly.

Set up the outdoor grill for direct-heat cooking over medium-low heat. Place a griddle, *plancha* or *piastra* suitable for use on an outdoor grill on the grill to preheat. Brush the griddle with oil. Cook the pork on the griddle for about 4–5 minutes on one side until golden, then turn over and cook for another 4–5 minutes until golden and cooked through (you may need to move the griddle to a cool part of the grill and pull the lid down to cook through).

To make the fennel salad, combine the fennel, parsley, olives, lemon segments, watercress, lemon olive oil and chives and place onto 4 serving plates. Top with the pork and serve immediately.

2 cups Japanese bread crumbs (panko)
1 handful of fresh sage leaves, roughly chopped
1/3 cup shredded Parmesan cheese
all-purpose flour, for dusting
4 x 10-ounce pork cutlets, trimmed
2 eggs, beaten
vegetable oil, for cooking

FENNEL SALAD
1 large fennel bulb, shaved
1 large handful of fresh Italian parsley
10 green olives, sliced
2 lemons, cut into segments
1 large handful of watercress
4 tablespoons lemon-infused extra-virgin olive oil
1/3 cup fresh chives, cut into 1¼-inch lengths

Around the corner from where I live, there was a popular little Portuguese chicken sandwich shop. I would often pop in and order a bite after a surf. It consisted of a fresh bun lightly toasted with chicken fillets bashed out to within an inch of their life and grilled with piri piri sauce and served with lettuce and mayo – utterly delicious and addictive. Since then, the little shop has gone so I have resorted to making my own... so this is my recipe.

piri piri chicken sandwiches

SERVES 4

**4 boneless, skinless chicken
  breast halves, pounded to
  flatten a bit**
2 tablespoons olive oil
butter, for the rolls
4 French rolls or burger buns, split
**¼ cup good-quality aïoli or
  mayonnaise**
**2 large handfuls of iceberg
  lettuce, torn**

PIRI PIRI SAUCE
6–12 small red arbol chiles
2 garlic cloves, coarsely chopped
½ teaspoon dried oregano
½ teaspoon paprika
¼ cup olive oil
2 tablespoons red wine vinegar

To make the piri piri sauce, preheat the broiler to medium and cook the chiles for 5 minutes, turning occasionally until softened. Coarsely chop and place into a saucepan with the garlic, 1 teaspoon sea salt, oregano, paprika, olive oil and vinegar and simmer for 3 minutes. Remove from heat and allow to cool, then process until smooth.

Marinate the chicken breasts in the olive oil and 2 tablespoons piri piri sauce for at least a few hours, if possible.

Set up the outdoor grill for direct-heat cooking over high heat. Scrape off the excess marinade and place the chicken on the grill. Cook for 2 minutes or until golden and marked on one side, then turn over and repeat (if you need to cook longer, move the chicken to a cooler part of the grill).

Butter the rolls and grill lightly until lightly golden. Remove from heat and top the roll bases with the aïoli or mayonnaise, chicken, some piri piri sauce and lettuce. Season with salt and pepper. Cover with the roll tops and serve right away.

The treacle was created by a very well known London bartender called Dick Bradsell. To this day he still works behind the bar creating some of the world's most popular contemporary classics. This drink is a twist on another classic cocktail called an Old Fashioned. It is the ideal accompanying drink to the rum and coke ribs (see recipe p56) or anything with a rich barbecue taste to it.

the treacle

SERVES 4–6

7 ounces golden rum
4 ounces unfiltered apple juice
½ ounce honey water (see note)
12 dashes of Angostura Bitters

Put all the ingredients into a pitcher with ice and stir slowly to combine. Pour into glasses.

GLASS: Large old-fashioned
GARNISH: Orange wedge
NOTE: Honey water is one part honey to one part hot water.

A whisky mac is a great structured drink for those who love the taste of a Scotch whisky. You could even add a little mint to complement the whisky. It also goes well with a lamb tagine (see recipe p47).

whisky mac

SERVES 4

1¼ ounces Scotch whisky (Famous Grouse works well)
2½ ounces Stones ginger wine

Put all the ingredients into a pitcher with ice and stir slowly to combine. Pour into glasses.

GLASS: Large old-fashioned
GARNISH: Orange twist (optional)
NOTE: Look for Stones ginger wine in large liquor retailers.

For lovers of tequila, this is a very refreshing drink with a hint of juice and fizz to cap it off. It's very easy to make and you can add mint or even some rich berries to add more flavor to it. It's a great match with the piri piri chicken sandwich (see recipe p79).

paloma

SERVES 4

Put the tequila, grapefruit juice, lime juice and sugar syrup into a pitcher with ice and stir to combine. Moisten the rim of the glasses with the lime and dip the rims into the salt. Divide the tequila mixture between the glasses and top with soda.

GLASS: Highball
GARNISH: Grapefruit wedge.
NOTE: Sugar syrup is equal parts sugar and water — place in a saucepan over medium heat and bring just to a boil, ensuring the sugar is dissolved. Set aside to cool.

7 ounces tequila
7 ounces pink grapefruit juice
2 ounces lime juice
1¼ ounces sugar syrup (see note)
salt, for glass rims
2 fluid ounces chilled club soda

This drink is rumored to date back as far as 1732 at the Schuylkill Fishing Club in Pennsylvania, when they were celebrating the welcome of ladies to the annual Christmas party. The rumor is a strong punch was created at the "Fish House" for all to enjoy. These days the drink is diluted with fruit and juice.

fish house punch

MAKES ABOUT 1 QUART

Put all the ingredients into a carafe with ice and stir well to combine.

GLASS: Highball
GARNISH: Mint sprigs, orange slices and maraschino cherries
NOTE: Sugar syrup is equal parts sugar and water — place in a saucepan over medium heat and bring just to a boil, ensuring the sugar is dissolved. Set aside to cool.

8 ounces Jamaican rum
4 ounces brandy
4 ounces lemon juice
3 ounces sugar syrup (see note)
8 ounces unfiltered apple juice
4 ounces guava juice or nectar
10 dashes of Angostura Bitters

lazy days

There's nothing more satisfying than firing up the grill on a sunny day and having your family or friends over for a feed, some drinks and to share a few laughs. The recipes in this chapter are all pretty much fun and designed to be shared with a minimum of fuss, and to actually get your guests involved in putting it together with you. I love making steak sandwiches or wraps and putting all the ingredients out and letting everyone create their own. Well, less for me to do…

Turkish-style stuffed flatbreads, gözlemes are great fun to make (well, I think so) and everyone loves them. This version is made with ground beef and finished with feta cheese and spinach leaves and lashings of lemon juice. I have tried it with lamb, chicken, beef and vegetarian options and they all taste delicious. I'll let you decide which is your favorite variation.

grilled gözlemes

SERVES 4

scant 1 cup plain yogurt
pinch of salt
2 cups self-rising flour
6 ounces ground beef
2 tablespoons olive oil, plus extra
  for cooking
1 garlic clove, minced
pinch of ground cumin
pinch of red pepper flakes
4 tablespoons tomato juice
1¾ cups baby spinach or
  Swiss chard
4 ounces feta cheese, crumbled
¼ cup butter, melted (optional)
lemon wedges, to serve

Beat the yogurt and salt together in large bowl until smooth. Gradually stir in the flour until you have a stiff dough. Tip onto a lightly floured work surface and gradually knead the dough, incorporating any remaining flour until the dough is soft and only slightly sticky. Transfer to a clean bowl and let stand, covered, for 30 minutes.

Cook the ground beef with the olive oil in a skillet over medium-high heat for about 2 minutes, or until browned all over. Add the garlic, cumin, pepper flakes and tomato juice and cook for another 1–2 minutes or until the mixture is dry. Remove from the heat, place the mixture in a colander and leave to cool and drain.

On a floured work surface, split the dough into 4 equal balls. Roll each piece of dough into a 12-inch circle.

Place a quarter of the spinach over half of each circle, sprinkle a quarter of the feta cheese over, then add a quarter of the beef mixture and season with salt and pepper. Fold the dough over and seal the edges with a fork. Repeat with the remaining dough and ingredients.

Set up the outdoor grill for direct-heat cooking over medium heat. Place a griddle, *plancha* or *piastra* suitable for use on an outdoor grill on the grill to preheat. Brush one side of each gözleme with olive oil and cook on the griddle until the base is golden. Brush the top side with olive oil, then turn over and cook until golden. Brush with the butter, if using, cut into 4 pieces and serve with lemon wedges.

This is a no-mess and no-stress recipe that I love for its sheer simplicity. Take some Asian vegetables such as bok choy or Chinese broccoli, get a lovely piece of any type of fish (that you've just bought or have been fortunate enough to catch yourself), then douse it all with a delicious sauce, wrap it all in aluminum foil and pop it onto the grill for 10 minutes. It puts the fun back into cooking as it allows you the time to do other things like topping off drinks, making sure the music is just right or just simply catching up on what your friends or family have been doing lately... now that is what outdoor grilling is all about.

salmon parcels with ginger, soy & bok choy

SERVES 4

Lay 4 large pieces of heavy-duty foil on a work surface and place half a bok choy in the center of each piece, then top with a salmon fillet, some ginger, some green onion and chile.

Set up the outdoor grill for direct-heat cooking over medium heat. Combine the soy, fish sauce, garlic, rice wine, cilantro root and stem and sesame oil and pour over the salmon. Quickly wrap the fish up so you don't lose any of the sauce and seal tightly.

Place the packets on the grill and cook for about 10 minutes or until the salmon is cooked to your liking.

Open up the foil (be careful of the steam) and serve immediately with the extra green onion strips and cilantro, if you like.

2 bok choy heads, cut in half and washed, or other Asian green
4 x 6-ounce salmon fillets (skinless)
1½ inch piece fresh ginger, julienned
3 green onions, cut into thin strips, plus extra to garnish
1 red serrano chile, cut into thin strips
½ cup soy sauce
1 tablespoon Asian fish sauce
2 garlic cloves, crushed
3 tablespoons shaoxing rice wine
1 tablespoon finely chopped fresh cilantro root and stem
½ teaspoon sesame oil
1 small handful fresh cilantro sprigs, to garnish (optional)

I was lucky enough to visit Japan a few years ago and I fell in love with the country – the people, the culture, the fashion and, of course, the food. I think Japanese food would have to be my favorite cuisine in the world: I love the attention to detail, the restraint and the respect they have for food and that they love using the best quality ingredients.

I remember trying these Japanese pancakes which are sold there as a street snack. They use a variety of ingredients in them – I've included scallops and shiitake mushrooms in mine as I love that flavor combination, but feel free to put in any seafood you like as the recipe works well with shrimp, fish or crab.

japanese pancakes with scallops & shiitake mushrooms

SERVES 4

scant ¾ cup all-purpose flour

2 tablespoons mirin (Japanese cooking wine)

1 teaspoon salt

2 eggs

12 scallops, thinly sliced

1 cup thinly sliced shiitake mushrooms

3⅓ cups shredded Chinese cabbage

4 green onions, chopped

4 tablespoons Japanese mayonnaise (see note)

4 tablespoons tonkatsu sauce (see note)

2 sheets nori, finely shredded

Set up the outdoor grill for direct-heat cooking over high heat. Place a cast-iron skillet or griddle suitable for use on an outdoor grill on the grill to preheat. Combine the flour, mirin, salt, eggs and ½ cup water in a large bowl. Stir in the scallops, mushrooms, cabbage and green onions.

Grease the skillet with vegetable oil. Spoon a quarter of the pancake mixture into the pan. Spread the mixture out to form a 6-inch circle. Cook for about 2–3 minutes or until lightly browned. Flip the pancake and cook for another 2 minutes. Repeat with the remaining batter.

To serve, drizzle the Japanese mayonnaise and tonkatsu sauce over the top of each pancake. Top with shredded nori.

NOTE: Japanese mayonnaise is an authentic egg and rice vinegar mayonnaise. Tonkatsu sauce is a thick, fruity brown sauce essential for pancakes and fried, crumbed Japanese dishes. Both are available in squeeze bottles from Asian stores and some supermarkets.

The most fun I've had while filming a TV show was last year when I spent the day with my business partner/chef Daniel Vaughan and his good friend, comedian Tim Smith. We were filming in their backyard in Melbourne and cooking in the wood-fired oven – I tell you everything tastes better once it has had a blasting in there. We cooked pizzas, the hairs on our arms (you have to watch out for the intense heat) and this dish here, which Daniel came up with. It's his version of sardines on toast, with a little inspiration from the Spanish with the use of some smoked paprika and some gorgeous sherry vinegar. This recipe has been adapted to be cooked on the outdoor grill.

spanish-style sardines on toast

SERVES 4

1 red bell pepper
½ red onion, roughly chopped
8 cherry tomatoes, halved
2 garlic cloves, sliced
1 large red serrano chile, quartered
    lengthwise
2 tablespoons olive oil, plus extra
    for brushing
1 teaspoon smoked paprika
1 tablespoon sherry vinegar
1 ounce feta cheese, crumbled
4 tablespoons roughly chopped
    fresh Italian parsley
4 whole fresh sardines, butterflied
4 slices of fresh Italian bread

Set up the outdoor grill for direct-heat cooking over high heat. Grill the bell pepper, turning occasionally, for 15–20 minutes or until the skin turns black. Remove from the grill and cool. Peel, seed and chop.

Place the onion, cherry tomatoes, garlic and chile, keeping each separate, in a mesh grill pan and cook with a touch of olive oil until softened and starting to color. Set aside the garlic and chile in separate bowls. Mix together the cooked garlic, olive oil, paprika and sherry vinegar to make a vinaigrette.

Combine the chopped pepper, onion, cherry tomatoes, crumbled feta and chopped parsley in a bowl and toss with a little olive oil and a little salt and pepper.

Brush the sardines with a little olive oil and place on the grill and sear on both sides. Season and cook until golden and cooked through, about 2 minutes on each side.

Brush the bread with a little olive oil and grill lightly. Top the bread with the warm pepper salad and chile, then place the sardines across the top. Dress with the sherry vinaigrette.

Ahhh, romesco sauce – I could eat it by the bucket load. It is such a good accompaniment but also so good by itself with some good-quality bread. Romesco sauce is a Spanish sauce made from roasted peppers, hazelnuts, garlic, vinegar and olive oil – very easy to make and well worth it.

I have teamed it here with grilled shrimp in the shell as you always get more flavor in your shrimp if you cook them still in the shell, as long as your friends and family don't mind peeling them, and if they do, find new friends (family might be a bit harder to replace, though). It also works well with any piece of fish, chicken or lamb you decide to throw on the outdoor grill. Serve with fresh bread.

shrimp with spanish romesco sauce

SERVES 4

Set up the outdoor grill for direct-heat cooking over high heat. To make the Romesco sauce, cook the peppers on the grill, turning occasionally, for 15–20 minutes or until the skin turns black. Remove from the grill and cool. Peel, seed and chop. Blend the pepper flesh, garlic, hazelnuts, roll and vinegar in a food processor. With the motor running, add the olive oil slowly so the sauce thickens. Season with salt and pepper.

Cook the shrimp, using a mesh grill pan if desired, for 2–3 minutes on each side or until changed in color and just cooked through. Serve with Romesco sauce on the side.

20 raw head-on jumbo shrimp,
  unpeeled

SPANISH ROMESCO SAUCE
3 red bell peppers
4 garlic cloves
1 cup hazelnuts, toasted
  and skins removed
1 sourdough roll, cut into
  4 pieces
½ cup sherry vinegar
1¼ cups extra-virgin olive oil

I just love cooking these little snacks as a starter. I like to think of them as the grown-up version of potato wedges with sweet chile and sour cream. Whoever came up with that combination deserves a medal. These cakes work well with shrimp, crayfish and even roast chicken but I especially like them with crabmeat. Enjoy!

crab & sweet corn cakes

SERVES 4

8 ounces cooked crabmeat

2 green onions, thinly sliced

1 red serrano chile, finely chopped

1 tablespoon roughly chopped
   fresh cilantro leaves

½ cup all-purpose flour

½ cup cornstarch

2 eggs, beaten

½ cup canned corn kernels, drained

⅔ cup crème fraîche or sour cream,
   to serve

sweet chile sauce, to serve (see note)

lime wedges, to serve

Lightly mix the crab, green onions, chile and cilantro in a bowl and season with salt and freshly ground black pepper.

Sift the flour and cornstarch into a separate bowl. Add ⅔ cup cold water and the eggs and whisk until smooth. Stir in the crab mixture and corn kernels. The mixture should have the consistency of heavy cream.

Set up the outdoor grill for direct-heat cooking over medium-high heat. Place a griddle, *plancha* or *piastra* suitable for use on an outdoor grill on the grill to preheat. Grease the griddle with some oil. Spoon small amounts of the batter onto the griddle and cook for 3 minutes on each side or until golden. Serve with crème fraîche, sweet chile sauce and lime wedges.

NOTE: Thai-style sweet chile sauce can be found in the Asian section of large supermarkets.

This is my type of food to serve when grilling outdoors — wraps. These days you can find fresh tortillas at most supermarkets and they make a welcome change from the standard sandwich bread. The sky is the limit when it comes to filling them, from vegetarian chili beans, chicken, fish and, of course, steak teamed with your favorite sauces and vegetables. This is a simple Mexican version that includes a recipe for chili beans, or you can just substitute with canned ones if you can't be bothered making your own. I sometimes buy the canned ones and just thin them down with some Mexican salsa as they can be a bit thick.

grilled steak wraps with chili beans

SERVES 4

2 tablespoons olive oil

1 large onion, chopped

2 garlic cloves, crushed

2 jalapeño chiles, seeds removed and chopped

1 tablespoon ground cumin

1 tablespoon paprika

pinch of pure chile powder

1 can (14 ounces) diced tomatoes

1 can (14 ounces) red kidney beans, rinsed and drained

2 x 8-ounce sirloin steaks

8 flour tortillas

1 avocado, diced

sour cream, to serve

1 large handful of fresh cilantro or Italian parsley leaves

½ cup shredded Cheddar cheese

Heat half the olive oil in a skillet and cook the onion, garlic and chiles until softened. Add the spices and heat until fragrant. Stir in the tomatoes and ½ cup of water and mix well. Simmer for 15 minutes, or until the sauce has reduced and is thick. Add the kidney beans and season with salt and pepper.

Set up the outdoor grill for direct-heat cooking over high heat. Rub the steak with the remaining oil and season with salt and pepper. Place the steak onto the grill and cook for 3–4 minutes on each side (or until cooked to your liking), then remove and let rest for 5 minutes before slicing across the grain.

Lightly grill the tortillas.

To serve, spread the bean mixture down the center of each tortilla, then top with steak slices, avocado, sour cream, cilantro and shredded cheese. Fold into thirds and serve immediately.

This is a very simple version of green mango salad, or *som tum*, as it is called in Thailand and it works well with seafood of any type. You can make it as spicy as you like by adjusting the amount of chile. A green mango is an underripe mango hence the fruit hasn't had time to ripen, so you have something of a tart-tasting fruit. On its own, it is not all that appealing, which is why you always see it in recipes as either finely sliced, or shredded to allow it to be palatable. Finely cutting the fruit also helps soak up the delicious dressing and really carry those flavors into the dish. Plus, I love the texture of the mango when it is green. If you can't find green mangoes, use green papaya or even apple or cucumber.

arctic char with simple green mango salad

SERVES 4

To make the dressing, put the lime zest and juice, sugar, vinegar, oil, and soy into a small bowl and whisk until combined.

Combine 1 tablespoon of the sesame seeds, and the bean sprouts and cilantro in another bowl and add the mango. Toss with half of the dressing.

Set up the outdoor grill for direct-heat cooking over high heat. Place a griddle, *plancha* or *piastra* suitable for use on an outdoor grill on the grill to preheat. Coat the fish in peanut oil and place, skin side down, on the griddle. Cook for 2–3 minutes on both sides, or until it is almost cooked through to the center but is still pink, then let rest for a few minutes.

Place the mango salad on top of the fish, sprinkle with the remaining sesame seeds and spoon the extra dressing over each piece of fish. Season with sea salt and cracked black pepper and serve.

2 tablespoons sesame seeds, toasted
1 cup bean sprouts, trimmed
1 small handful of cilantro leaves
1 green mango, peeled and finely shredded
4 x 6-ounce arctic char fillets
peanut oil, for cooking

DRESSING
2 limes, zest finely grated and juiced
1 tablespoon light brown sugar
2 tablespoon rice vinegar
1 tablespoon peanut oil
1 tablespoon light soy sauce

I think squid has yet to be fully embraced as a seafood of choice for home cooking. It is always the biggest seller on any restaurant's menu, especially when coated in flour, deep-fried and tossed with chile and salt or the like. When it comes to home cooking though, I think it gets overlooked – probably because it can look a bit daunting to someone who has never cooked squid before. Not only is it easy to prepare, it's really easy to cook so there's no reason not to add it to your grill repertoire.

chile-spiced grilled squid with salsa

SERVES 4

If you want to score the flesh of the bodies to make it curl up, then lightly run your knife across the flesh in a zigzag pattern or just cut into strips. Cut the squid bodies into 2-inch pieces.

Set up the outdoor grill for direct-heat cooking over high heat. Place a griddle, *plancha* or *piastra* suitable for use on an outdoor grill on the grill to preheat. Mix the olive oil, pepper flakes, cilantro, garlic, cumin and ground coriander in a bowl and season with salt and pepper. Toss with the squid, then place the squid onto the griddle and cook for about 1 minute, or until opaque.

Mix Donnie's salsa with the olive oil and serve with the squid.

¾ **pound squid bodies and tentacles, cleaned**
2 **tablespoons olive oil**
1 **teaspoon red pepper flakes**
1 **tablespoon chopped fresh cilantro root and stem**
1 **garlic clove, minced**
pinch of ground cumin
pinch of ground coriander
1 **cup Donnie's famous tomato salsa (see recipe opposite)**
2 **tablespoons extra-virgin olive oil**

This recipe is from my very good friend, Donnie St Pierre. He's famous for coaching the US Olympic freestyle ski team, and also for this salsa. Here's his reply to my request for his recipe:

"Where to begin... Let me say that I feel quite strange writing to you about anything to do with food. It's important to understand there appears to be no right or wrong way of making this and every Mexican restaurant whether in Mexico or Southwestern USA makes it in their own special or unique way. Chop the red onion, chile and garlic fine to avoid overpowering the salsa. Add chopped cilantro and lime juice to taste. I prefer it served chilled but obviously this would be an American thing as refrigeration and cool weather are scarce in Mexico."

donnie's famous tomato salsa

SERVES 4

6 vine-ripened tomatoes,
   roughly chopped
1 small red onion, very
   finely chopped
1 handful of fresh cilantro leaves,
   finely chopped
1 garlic clove, finely chopped
1 Thai chile, seeded and
   finely chopped
juice of 1 lime

Combine all ingredients in a bowl and season to taste with salt.

Donnie's tip for making salsa: The method to bring these ingredients together is anyone's choice depending on the texture and how much garlic and chile they can stand. I tend to like the tomatoes hand-chopped to avoid too soupy a salsa that can be hard to collect on a corn chip. But I've had some really great runny salsa.

This dish is my version of fast food – I reckon it takes no longer than 15 minutes tops, from the time you unpack your groceries to the time it takes to sit down and eat it. In the time it takes to toast your pine nuts, cook your tuna to medium-rare and wilt some radicchio, the kids are only halfway through their fave TV show and you are wondering why life can't always be this easy... The thing to remember here is that buying good-quality tuna (or any other type of fish or seafood) is important as the fish is center stage for this dish. The radicchio di Treviso is an Italian lettuce with a bitter flavor so the sweetness of the raisins and the apple balsamic vinegar balance this out.

tuna with raisins, pine nuts & radicchio

SERVES 4

4 x 6-ounce tuna steaks
2 heads of radicchio di Treviso or
    red Belgian endive
olive oil, for cooking
scant ½ cup lemon-infused extra
    virgin olive oil
scant ¼ cup apple balsamic vinegar
    (see note)
¼ cup pine nuts, toasted
¼ cup golden raisins
1 handful of fresh Italian parsley

Set up the outdoor grill for direct-heat cooking over medium heat. Place a griddle, *plancha* or *piastra* suitable for use on an outdoor grill on the grill to preheat. Season the tuna steaks with coarsely ground black pepper and salt.

Break the radicchio into individual leaves and toss in a little olive oil. Scatter the leaves onto the griddle and cook briefly until they start to wilt. Toss the radicchio while still warm in a large bowl with the lemon-infused olive oil, apple balsamic, pine nuts, raisins and parsley and season with salt and pepper.

Cook the tuna on the griddle for 2 minutes each side for rare to medium-rare. Serve with the salad.

NOTE: Look for apple balsamic vinegar in specialty food stores.

This is the one of the nicest ways to eat a piece of fish cooked on the outdoor grill. You do, however, need to prepare this dish a few days in advance as the fish needs time to cure in the miso paste, wine and sugar mixture. Miso is a great flavor enhancer for meat or seafood when used as a marinade but be careful as each paste varies from brand to brand and some are saltier than others. You can find this dish on many Japanese menus.

japanese miso-marinated fish

SERVES 4

To make the paste, combine the miso, ginger, mirin, sake and sugar until the sugar has dissolved. Place about a third of the paste on the bottom of a baking dish, then top with the salmon. Cover with the rest of the paste and leave, covered, in the fridge for 3 days to marinate.

Set up the outdoor grill for direct-heat cooking over medium-high heat. Place a griddle, *plancha* or *piastra* suitable for use on an outdoor grill on the grill to preheat. Take the fish out of the dish and wipe off all excess marinade with a damp cloth. Cook on the oiled griddle for 4 minutes on each side and serve with pickled ginger, if you like, and garnish with the green onion.

4 x 6-ounce Atlantic salmon
   fillets (skin on)
pickled ginger, to serve (optional)
2 green onions, green part only,
   julienned

MISO PASTE
1¾ cups white miso paste
   (saikyo miso)
6 slices fresh ginger
1 tablespoon mirin (Japanese
   cooking wine)
5 teaspoons sake
1½ tablespoons sugar

This is a great summer recipe using the flavors of the Mediterranean. Ratatouille is traditionally a vegetable stew from the south of France but I have adapted this recipe for the outdoor grill. Herbs de Provence is a special herb mixture that can be purchased at good delicatessens or spice shops and typically contains rosemary, marjoram, basil, bay leaf thyme and lavender. Never add it after cooking as it has a very strong flavor.

grilled lamb brochettes with provençal herbs & ratatouille

SERVES 4

2 tablespoons herbs de Provence
3 garlic cloves, crushed
about 1¼ cups olive oil
2 pounds lamb leg (ask your butcher to dice into 1-inch pieces)
16 bay leaves

RATATOUILLE
1 red bell pepper
1 green bell pepper
1 red onion
2 zucchini
1 small eggplant
1½ cups cherry tomatoes, cut in halves
about 1¼ cups olive oil
1 large handful of fresh basil leaves
1 tablespoon seeded mustard
2 teaspoons honey
3 tablespoons red wine vinegar

Combine the herbs de Provence, garlic and olive oil in a baking dish. Add the lamb, cover and refrigerate overnight to marinate. If you are using wooden skewers, you'll also need to soak these in water overnight.

Set up the outdoor grill for direct-heat cooking over high heat. To make the ratatouille, cut all the vegetables except the cherry tomatoes into large bite-sized pieces. Toss in ⅔ cup of the olive oil and season with salt and pepper. Cook in a mesh grill pan for 10–20 minutes, turning occasionally, or until tender. Place in a bowl with the tomatoes and basil. Mix together the mustard, honey, vinegar and remaining olive oil in a separate bowl and season, then set aside.

Place about 4 lamb cubes on each skewer, alternating with the bay leaves. Grill for 10–15 minutes, turning occasionally, for medium, or until done to your liking. Set aside to rest.

To serve, drizzle half of the dressing over the ratatouille and the rest of the dressing over the lamb.

One country I really want to visit is Greece and its islands. It looks beautiful and I can't wait to eat some octopus from their waters, or lamb from the fields. This is a simple little recipe to throw together on the grill. It has some wonderful flavors that I love — zucchini, anchovies, garlic and feta, not to mention the lamb. I have used lamb chops here as I really do think it is a fantastic cut of meat to cook on the grill. It's also pretty hard to get it wrong when cooking chops.

greek-style lamb chops with zucchini, anchovy & feta dressing

SERVES 4

In a bowl, combine the garlic, 2 tablespoons of the oil and dried oregano and season with sea salt and cracked black pepper. Use this mixture to marinate the lamb chops for at least 30 minutes.

Set up the outdoor grill for direct-heat cooking over high heat. Cook the lamb for 2–3 minutes each side or until cooked to your liking.

Coat the zucchini slices with oil and some sea salt and cracked black pepper and cook on the grill in a mesh grill pan until golden. Toss in a bowl with the anchovies, pine nuts, feta, pepper flakes, remaining olive oil, fresh oregano, lemon juice and olives.

Serve the lamb chops with the warm zucchini salad.

2 garlic cloves, finely chopped
6 tablespoons extra-virgin olive oil
1 teaspoon dried oregano
8 lamb loin chops
2 large zucchini, cut into ¼-inch thick slices
3 anchovy fillets, torn into pieces
1 tablespoon pine nuts, toasted
3 ounces feta cheese, crumbled
pinch of red pepper flakes
1 small handful of fresh oregano leaves
juice of ½ lemon
¼ cup Ligurian olives

When I started to plan this book, I asked a lot of people what they loved cooking on the outdoor grill at home and, surprisingly, most of the men said they love to cook a butterflied lamb leg. I would have thought it would have been a steak or sausages that got the vote. So I thought I'd include my favorite way of cooking a lamb leg on the outdoor grill and that is with harissa. I have included the recipe for making your own harissa paste here, but you can buy prepared harissa at a specialty food store, if you like.

grilled leg of lamb with harissa & minted yogurt

SERVES 4

1 butterflied leg of lamb, about
    4 pounds
herbed couscous, to serve (optional)

HARISSA
1 red bell pepper
8 red serrano chiles, deseeded
3 garlic cloves
1 bunch fresh cilantro
1 teaspoon caraway seeds, toasted
2 teaspoons coriander seeds, toasted
about 2/3 cup olive oil

DRESSING
1 cup plain yogurt
1 bunch of fresh mint
1 garlic clove

Set up the outdoor grill for direct-heat cooking over high heat. To make the harissa, cook the bell pepper on the grill, turning occasionally, for 15–20 minutes or until the skin turns black. Remove from the grill and let cool. Peel, seed and roughly chop the flesh. Let the coals cool a bit or reduce the grill heat to medium.

Place the chiles, garlic, cilantro, caraway seeds, coriander seeds and bell pepper in a food processor and blend, slowly adding the oil until a thick paste forms. Season with salt and pepper and smear the paste over the lamb on both sides.

Grill the lamb, covered, for 8–10 minutes on each side for medium-rare. Cook for a few minutes longer if you prefer your lamb more cooked. Remove and let rest in a warm place for 10–15 minutes.

To make the dressing, blend the yogurt with the mint and garlic and add a pinch of salt. Slice the lamb and serve with the dressing and some herbed couscous.

I was a vegetarian for about four years when I was 19. I needed a change in lifestyle so I did a three-day course on self-improvement and came back changed for the better – I didn't touch any alcohol or meat for the next four years. I really embraced vegetarian cooking and used legumes, nuts, fruit and vegetables to create wonderful meals. I took it very seriously and learnt a lot about health and wellbeing in that time. However, I did start to crave meat again and now I have a varied diet. This recipe uses one of my favorite ingredients to cook on the outdoor grill, haloumi, a firm, tangy, Greek-style cheese. I have added chorizo to spice things up a bit, but you can leave it out and it will still taste wonderful.

grilled haloumi with roasted peppers, chickpeas & chorizo

SERVES 4

4 red bell peppers
2 Spanish-style cured chorizo
   sausages, cut into ¼-inch slices
pinch of smoked paprika
4 tablespoons extra-virgin olive oil
1 tablespoon sherry or red
   wine vinegar
1 handful fresh Italian parsley
1 can (14 ounces) chickpeas,
   rinsed and drained
8 ounces haloumi cheese, cut
   into ¼-inch slices
olive oil, for cooking
pinch of red pepper flakes
juice of 1 lemon

Set up the outdoor grill for direct-heat cooking over high heat. Cook the bell peppers on the grill, turning occasionally, for 15–20 minutes or until the skin turns black. Remove from the grill and let cool. Peel, seed and cut the flesh into strips.

Cook the chorizo on the grill until slightly blackened on each side. Add the chorizo to a bowl with the paprika, olive oil, sherry vinegar, parsley, bell peppers and chickpeas.

Meanwhile, lightly coat the haloumi with oil and cook on the grill for 1–2 minutes until golden on each side. Season with sea salt, pepper flakes and lemon juice. Add the grilled haloumi to the chorizo mixture and toss gently to combine.

NOTE: Haloumi has a higher melting point than many other cheeses, so it won't melt when you grill it.

Merguez sausages are from North Africa but have been adopted by the French, especially in the south. Traditionally they are made with lamb but beef could be substituted if you like. I find the best accompaniments are a homemade chutney such as date or tomato, and some flatbread (or any type of bread). You could also flatten them to make patties and top them with a yogurt sauce – really easy and super-tasty.

homemade merguez sausages

SERVES 4

Combine the lamb, fat, harissa, cinnamon, garlic, fennel seeds, mint and salt in a bowl and knead for 5 minutes. Place in the refrigerator overnight to marinate.

Set up an outdoor grill for direct-heat cooking over medium heat. Place a griddle, *plancha* or *piastra* suitable for use on an outdoor grill on the grill to preheat. Form the mixture into sausage shapes and cook on the griddle for 8–10 minutes, turning occasionally, until cooked through. Serve with onion and tomato.

NOTE: Ask your butcher for a piece of lamb fat.

14 ounces lean ground lamb
3½ ounces ground lamb fat
    (see note)
1 tablespoon harissa paste (see
    recipe p119 or store-bought)
1 teaspoon ground cinnamon
4 garlic cloves, crushed
¼ teaspoon crushed fennel seeds
1 teaspoon dried mint leaves
2 tablespoons sea salt
1 red onion, cut into wedges
1 tomato, cut into bite-sized pieces

I traveled up the coast of Portugal a few years back and I absolutely loved it. It was the end of a five-week road trip (I love the European autobahns with no speed limit) with my partner Astrid before we had our children. We took in Belgium, Austria, Italy, France and Spain, and Portugal was the perfect place to finish that vacation. We needed to get away from people and expensive restaurants so from Lisbon we traveled along the coast and spent a few nights in little fishing villages way off the tourist route. We got to experience some amazing food and old fishing practices still carried out today. These burgers may not be traditional but they are in honor of the relaxing last few days I spent on the magnificent coastline there. They are great to serve with some crusty rolls, aïoli and salad.

portuguese burgers

SERVES 4

2 tablespoons Spanish sweet paprika
1 tablespoon ground cumin
1 tablespoon ground coriander
2/3 cup olive oil
2⅓ pounds coarsely ground
  pork shoulder
1 teaspoon pure chile powder
3 garlic cloves, minced
2 tablespoons sea salt
1 tablespoon ground black pepper
2 eggs
1 cup fresh bread crumbs
4 French rolls, split
store-bought tomato chutney,
  to serve
store-bought aïoli, to serve
  (optional)
baby romaine lettuce, to serve

Gently cook the paprika, cumin, coriander and oil in a heavy-bottomed skillet over medium heat for 1–2 minutes or until fragrant. When cool, add the pork shoulder, chile powder, garlic, salt, pepper, eggs and bread crumbs and knead for 2–3 minutes until well combined.

Set up the outdoor grill for direct-heat cooking over medium heat. Form the mixture into about 4 patties and cook for 5 minutes on each side, or until just cooked through.

Lightly grill the rolls and serve the patties on the bread with some tomato chutney, aïoli and lettuce on the side.

I remember my first trip to Bali about 20 years ago – it was the first time I had ever used my passport since my mum and dad took me on a trip around the world when I was one, so I was thrilled to explore a different culture and try their cuisine. I can remember my first taste of *gado gado*, *mi goreng* and chicken satay cooked on the side of the road and *nasi goreng* for breakfast. The one thing that stood out the most was the grilled corncobs cooked in the little side streets. Locals selling corn on their makeshift bikes with the grill attached. Talk about the simple things in life: grilled corn with chile butter and a cold Bintang beer, watching the sun set... nothing better!

grilled corn with chile & lime

SERVES 4

Place the corn ears in cold water and soak for 10–20 minutes. Peel back (but don't remove) the husks from the cobs. Remove and discard the silk, then bring the husks back over the cob.

Set up the outdoor grill for direct-heat cooking over medium heat. Grill the corn for 15–20 minutes, turning frequently, until the corn husks are dry and brown.

Meanwhile, combine the butter with the pepper flakes, cilantro, Tabasco and sea salt.

Peel back the husks, brush on the butter mixture liberally and cook for another minute on the grill until the husk blackens in places, then remove from the heat and baste on more butter. Serve with lime wedges.

4 ears of corn
½ cup butter, softened
1 teaspoon red pepper flakes
2 tablespoons chopped fresh cilantro leaves
Tabasco sauce, to taste (about 10-20 drops)
lime wedges, to serve

Mojo sauce originated in the Canary Islands and is now popular throughout the Caribbean and Cuba. It can be used as a marinade, dip or sauce to serve with pork as I've done here. When you are cooking the pork on the outdoor grill, make sure you don't have the heat too high, as the marinade has a quite a bit of sugar in it and so the chops may burn, although a little bit of caramelization is always nice, especially if you're teaming your chops with pineapple, lime and ginger. Serve with grilled corn with chile and lime (recipe opposite).

marinated pork chops with pineapple & ginger mojo

SERVES 4

4 pork chops

MARINADE
1½-inch piece fresh ginger, chopped
1 tablespoon ground coriander
½ teaspoon pure chile powder
2 garlic cloves
4 tablespoons tomato ketchup
2 tablespoons honey

PINEAPPLE & GINGER MOJO
¼ fresh pineapple, peeled and diced
1 cup candied ginger, finely chopped
½ cup coarsely chopped
   macadamia nuts
1 cup extra-virgin olive oil
juice of 4 limes
1 bunch of fresh cilantro, chopped
ground coriander, to taste

To make the marinade, blend the ginger, coriander, chile powder, garlic, ketchup and honey together to form a paste. Coat the pork chops in the marinade and refrigerate, covered, for at least 2 hours and up to 24 hours.

To make the mojo, combine the pineapple, candied ginger and macadamia nuts. Add the oil, lime juice and chopped cilantro. Season with salt and pepper and ground coriander.

Set up the outdoor grill for direct-heat cooking over medium-low heat. Cook the pork chops for 3–4 minutes on each side or until cooked through. Serve with the mojo.

It is so hard to cook something to everyone's taste. Take my brother Dave for instance, he has an aversion to fennel and also to any meat with fat running through it (I, on the other hand, love it). Now I am not having a go at him, he doesn't like it and that's fine, but when your brother is your business partner and toughest critic it can be hard coming up with dishes that he likes. That is where this dish comes in – Dave loves filet mignon and sirloin (if the fat is taken off) so this was designed as a no-nonsense dish that would please him, as well as the customers, and also the cooks in the kitchen. We have had this on and off at my restaurant, Hugo's Bar Pizza in Kings Cross, Sydney, for years. Quick to cook and a wonderful grilled dish for the warmer months...

quick steaks with green olive dressing & tomato salad

SERVES 4

To make the tomato salad, place the tomatoes, garlic, basil leaves, mineral water and olive oil into a bowl, season to taste with sea salt and cracked black pepper, then squeeze with your hand. Let stand for 10 minutes for the flavors to develop.

Set up the outdoor grill for direct-heat cooking over medium heat. To make the green olive dressing, sauté the onion with a little olive oil in a skillet for a minute, then add them to a bowl with the olives, lemon juice, celery, olive oil, sea salt, pepper and chopped parsley.

Brush the steaks with a little oil and season with salt and pepper. Then cook on the grill for 1–2 minutes on each side or until cooked to your liking.

Serve the steaks topped with some of the olive dressing, and the tomato salad on the side.

4 x 6-ounce sirloin steaks, pounded to flatten slightly
4 lemon wedges, to serve (optional)

TOMATO SALAD
30 cherry tomatoes, cut into quarters
2 garlic cloves, thinly sliced
10 fresh basil leaves, torn
½ cup sparkling mineral water
4 tablespoons extra-virgin olive oil

GREEN OLIVE DRESSING
3 teaspoons finely chopped onion
½ cup olive oil
½ cup roughly chopped green Sicilian olives
3 tablespoons lemon juice
½ celery rib, finely chopped
3 tablespoons chopped fresh Italian parsley

I've heard it said somewhere that "to be a great cook it's not what you put on the plate but what you leave off that matters". John Pye, a friend of mine from way back when we worked at Hugos at Sydney's Bondi Beach, has a great understanding of when it's time to use restraint when creating a dish such as this one. What could be simpler than a lovely piece of fish cooked on the outdoor grill and served with one of the yummiest accompaniments I have ever tried? So enjoy this simple relish as it works so well with any seafood or cuts of pork, or lamb or chicken you may wish to cook over some hot coals.

halibut steaks with spiced eggplant relish

SERVES 4

4 x 6-ounce halibut or salmon steaks
4 tablespoons extra-virgin olive oil
4 lime wedges, to serve

SPICED EGGPLANT RELISH
1 eggplant, diced into ¾-inch cubes
4 tablespoons olive oil
2 garlic cloves, finely chopped
2 shallots, chopped
4 anchovy fillets
4 tablespoons chopped fresh Italian
  parsley, plus extra whole leaves,
  to garnish
2 tablespoons capers, rinsed
2 tablespoons chile jam (see note)
2 tablespoons red wine vinegar

To make the spiced eggplant relish, preheat a heavy skillet over medium-high heat. Toss the eggplant in half the olive oil and cook in the skillet, stirring, until golden. Drain on paper towels.

Add the remaining olive oil to the skillet and fry the garlic and shallots over medium heat for 3–5 minutes or until golden. Add the anchovies, parsley, capers, chile jam, vinegar and eggplant and mix well. Cook for another 5 minutes over low heat until all flavors have mingled well, then season with salt and pepper.

Set up the outdoor grill for direct-heat cooking over high heat. Place a griddle, *plancha* or *piastra* suitable for use on an outdoor grill on the grill to preheat. Rub the fish with some olive oil and season with sea salt and cracked black pepper. Cook on the griddle for about 2–3 minutes on one side, then turn and cook for 2–3 minutes on the other side until just cooked through. Serve with the spiced eggplant relish and lime wedges to the side.

NOTE: Chile jam is a relish, available from delicatessens and gourmet food stores.

Sydney chef Peter Kuruvita has a wonderful relationship with seafood. I filmed with Pete a couple of times over the past few years and was lucky enough to be with him the day he made his version of chile crab. This dish is loosely based on Peter's recipe but I have made it with lobster as I think lobster needs all the help it can get to make it taste as good as a crab (sorry, I am a crab bloke from way back) and I couldn't possibly put another chile crab recipe in one of my cookbooks.

iron-skillet lobster with mirin & chile sauce

SERVES 4

Place the lobsters in the freezer for about 3–4 hours until they are immobilized (but not frozen), then remove the heads, and cut in half and remove the coral (mustard-looking part in the head). Cut the tails into 1-inch medallions with a cleaver or heavy kitchen knife.

Blend the chiles, ginger, cilantro, light soy, mirin, white wine, sesame oil, sweet chile sauce and garlic in a food processor until finely blended.

Set up the outdoor grill for direct-heat cooking over medium-high heat. Place a large cast-iron skillet on the grill to preheat. Add the lobster to the skillet and pour in the blended mixture. Cover the grill and cook for 5 minutes, or until the lobster turns orange and the flesh is just cooked through. Top with the green onions and fresh herbs and serve with jasmine rice and the iron-skillet Asian vegetables.

NOTE: Spiny lobsters from the Pacific or Caribbean are smaller than Maine lobsters and lack the large front claws.

2 live spiny lobsters, about
    1¾ pounds each
2 red serrano chiles, seeded
    and chopped
3¼-inch piece of fresh ginger, peeled
    and chopped
½ bunch of fresh cilantro including
    roots, chopped
1 cup light soy sauce
1 cup mirin (Japanese cooking wine)
½ cup dry white wine
1 tablespoon sesame oil
½ cup sweet chile sauce
2 garlic cloves, chopped
½ bunch green onions, cut
    into 2-inch lengths
1 large handful of mixed fresh
    herbs, such as mint, cilantro
    and Thai basil
steamed jasmine rice, to serve
iron-skillet Asian vegetables, to serve
    (see recipe opposite)

I love the fact that my outdoor grill at home has a wok burner (or an additional separate burner) on the side that allows me to either have a sauce simmering away to serve with grilled fish or meat, or, better still, how about stir-fried Asian dishes that you can cook outdoors? A cast-iron skillet set directly on the grill grate is a fine alternative to a wok. This is one of my favorite dishes to cook as a side dish to accompany anything from Southeast Asia.

iron-skillet asian vegetables

SERVES 4

about 2¼ pounds bok choy, Chinese cabbage or other Asian green
1 tablespoon brown bean sauce or soy sauce (see note)
1 tablespoon soft brown sugar
3 tablespoons peanut oil
8 garlic cloves, chopped
as many chiles as you can tolerate, sliced
2 tablespoons Asian fish sauce

Wash the bok choy several times, then cut into quarters.

Set up the outdoor grill for direct-heat cooking over high heat. Place a large cast-iron skillet on the grill to preheat.

Put the bok choy in a bowl, add the brown bean sauce, sugar, oil, garlic and chiles and mix to combine.

When you are satisfied that your skillet is red-hot, stand clear and pour the contents of the bowl into it. You should get a spectacular sizzling sound. When it dies down, stir madly for a minute or so, gradually adding the fish sauce. Once the greens have wilted, serve immediately.

NOTE: Brown bean sauce, made from fermented soybeans, can be found in jars in Asian supermarkets.

This dish is my version of *char kway teow*, which literally means fried flat noodles. I have eaten this many times in Singapore and Malaysia at the markets and stalls over there and I have to admit their version tastes slightly better than mine as they often cook it in pork fat and serve it with pork lard, which gives it its addictive flavor. I have opted for a fresher version here using peanut oil and the addition of shrimp, just because I love them. Make sure you wash it down with a cold Asian beer, preferably a Tiger, and you are onto a good thing.

malaysian noodles

SERVES 4

Place the noodles into a heatproof bowl and pour over some boiling water. Let stand for 5–10 minutes, then gently separate the noodles with your fingers. Drain and set aside.

Set up the outdoor grill for direct-heat cooking over high heat. Place a large cast-iron skillet on the grill to preheat. Add the oil, garlic, ginger and sambal to the skillet and cook for 1–2 minutes, or until fragrant. Toss in the sausages and green onions and cook for another minute.

Add the shrimp and stir-fry until just changing color, then stir in the pork and cook for another 2 minutes.

Combine the fish sauce and kecap manis and mix well. Pour into the pan and reduce until thick and sticky. Add the noodles, bean sprouts and chives and toss to coat. Serve immediately topped with peanuts.

NOTE: Sambal oelek is an Indonesian chile paste, available from Asian food stores.

Lap Cheong are dried Chinese pork sausages, usually smoked, seasoned and sweetened, available from the Asian section of larger supermarkets and Asian food stores.

Char sui pork is available from Chinese grill restaurants, many of which have a storefront for selling cooked meat.

1¼ pounds fresh flat rice noodles
2 tablespoons peanut oil
4 garlic cloves, chopped
¾-inch piece fresh ginger, finely grated
2 teaspoons sambal oelek (see note) or 2 small red chiles, chopped
2 Chinese sausages (lap cheong sausages), sliced (see note)
4 green onions, cut into 2-inch lengths
20 small raw shrimp, peeled and deveined with tails intact
6 ounces Chinese grilled pork (char sui), cut into thin slices (see note)
2 tablespoons Asian fish sauce
3 tablespoons kecap manis (sweet dark soy sauce)
1 cup bean sprouts
1 bunch garlic chives, cut into 1¼-inch lengths
¼ cup roasted peanuts

This method is great as it keeps the meat moist while giving it a fantastic flavor. You can also use one large whole roast chicken instead of four small chickens or poussins, if you like. Preserved lemons add an extra kick and freshness and can be purchased from specialty food stores — remember, use only the peel.

chicken with preserved lemon, chile & rosemary

SERVES 4

2 red serrano chiles, seeded
   and chopped
1 preserved lemon, rinsed
   and peel diced
1 garlic clove, finely chopped
4 rosemary sprigs, finely chopped
1 cup butter, softened
juice of 1 lemon
1 large handful of fresh parsley
   leaves, finely chopped
4 x 1-pound small chickens, poussins
   or game hens, butterflied
lime wedges, to serve
rosemary sprigs, to garnish

Put the chiles, preserved lemon peel, garlic, rosemary, butter, lemon juice and parsley in a bowl and mix well. Lift the skin of the chicken and push the flavored butter underneath. Refrigerate the chickens until the butter is firm.

Set up the outdoor grill for direct-heat cooking over medium heat. Place a griddle, *plancha* or *piastra* suitable for use on an outdoor grill on the grill to preheat. Cook the chickens, flesh side down, on the griddle for 6 minutes, then turn and cook for another 6 minutes, or until cooked through. Serve with lime wedges and garnish with the rosemary.

I can remember catching my first Spanish mackerel — well, it wasn't mine really, it was my brother-in-law Udo who managed to bring it in and it was nearly an Australian record. We were filming an episode for our fishing and cooking show called *Fish* and we had very little time allocated to fishing (that's TV for you) so it was always very stressful when we went out on a boat. We wanted to make sure we caught something otherwise it would be a very expensive waste of time. This time the stars were all aligned and Udo brought in this magnificent creature. It is one of the best fish in the ocean by far — perfect raw for sashimi but also equally as perfect slapped onto an outdoor grill as a lovely steak. Team it with a light salad or in this instance with braised tomato and fennel. Mackerel can stand up to strong flavors so the addition of olive tapenade here works really well.

spanish mackerel with tomato, fennel & caper berries

SERVES 4

To make the tapenade, combine the olives, parsley, lemon juice and oil.

Set up the outdoor grill for direct-heat cooking over medium-high heat. Place a griddle, *plancha* or *piastra* suitable for use on an outdoor grill on the grill to preheat. Brush the fennel and tomato with half the olive oil and cook on the griddle until golden, then place in a saucepan over medium heat with the fish broth, saffron and garlic and simmer for 20 minutes or until soft. Season with salt and pepper and finish with chopped parsley.

Brush the mackerel fillets with the remaining oil and place onto the griddle and cook on one side for a few minutes, then turn over and cook another 1–2 minutes, or until just cooked through.

Divide the tomato and fennel mixture among plates, then top with the fish, a spoonful of tapenade and some caper berries.

2 bulbs of fennel, roughly chopped
6 vine-ripened tomatoes, cut in half
3 tablespoons olive oil
½ cup fish broth or clam juice
pinch of saffron threads
2 garlic cloves, chopped
1 tablespoon chopped fresh
   Italian parsley
4 x 6-ounce Spanish mackerel fillets
4 tablespoons green olive tapenade
   (store bought or see recipe below)
12 caper berries

GREEN OLIVE TAPENADE
1 cup green olives, pitted and
   finely chopped
1 handful of fresh Italian parsley,
   finely chopped
2 tablespoons lemon juice
3 tablespoons olive oil

One of the best sandwiches in the world is this one – not even my famous shrimp roll can top it! You must try one to believe it. It is based on the chicken rolls you get in places like Sydney's Cabramatta which has a high concentration of Vietnamese residents, restaurants and bakeries (and we all know the Vietnamese bakeries are some of the best in the world: they were taught by the French after all!). I have adapted it slightly to be cooked on an outdoor grill but you could just as easily use roasted chicken from the night before or store-bought grilled chicken instead. The key here is the pickled carrot and onion and also the delicious flavored mayonnaise slathered onto the bread. Use the best-quality baguettes you can find.

vietnamese grilled chicken salad baguettes

SERVES 4

2 tablespoons white vinegar

1 teaspoon sugar

1 garlic clove, crushed

1 red arbol chile, finely chopped, or 1 teaspoon sambal oelek (see note)

1 large carrot, grated

1 white onion, finely sliced

4 boneless chicken breast halves (skin on)

4 tablespoons mayonnaise

1 tablespoon lime juice

½ teaspoon five-spice powder

2 baguettes, halved and sliced lengthwise (being careful to not cut all the way through)

1 handful of fresh cilantro leaves

4 tablespoons roasted and chopped cashews or peanuts

1 long red chile, finely chopped

Combine the vinegar, sugar, ½ teaspoon of salt, garlic and chile and mix well. Add the grated carrot and sliced onion, mix well and set aside.

Set up the outdoor grill for direct-heat cooking over medium-high heat. Place a griddle, *plancha* or *piastra* suitable for use on an outdoor grill on the grill to preheat. Place the chicken, skin side down, on the griddle and cook for 8 minutes or until the skin is golden. Turn over and continue cooking for 5 minutes or until cooked through. Allow to cool, then shred the meat.

Combine the mayonnaise with the lime juice and five-spice powder and mix well.

Lightly toast the baguettes on the griddle. Spread the mayonnaise mixture onto one side of the bread. Top with shredded chicken and then with the carrot and onion salad. Garnish the roll with chopped cilantro, nuts, and chile.

NOTE: Sambal oelek is an Indonesian chile paste, available from Asian markets.

I have been designing pizza toppings for years and the real secret to it is to take whatever is great with pasta and pop it onto a pizza (although I can't really fathom a ham and pineapple pasta dish — there is always one exception to the rule). This is a classic pasta sauce recipe that has all the flavors of Italy in spades — olives, capers, anchovies, basil, tomato and buffalo mozzarella. Yum! There is no need to do anything more to this, other than to add a bit of garlic and some chile, to make it special... oh and don't forget a good drizzle of olive oil once it is cooked.

puttanesca pizza

SERVES 4

To make the dough, put the yeast, sugar, salt and olive oil in a mixing bowl with 1 cup of warm water and stir gently. Let stand for 15 minutes for the yeast to activate (it will look foamy). Slowly stir in the flour and knead for about 5 minutes until the dough is smooth. Put in a lightly oiled bowl and leave in a warm place for about 30 minutes to an hour until doubled in size. Punch down the dough with one good punch. Divide the dough into four 6-ounce balls, then leave in a warm place until they have risen slightly.

Meanwhile, to make the tomato sauce, blend the tomatoes, peppercorns, oregano and a pinch of salt in a food processor.

Set up the outdoor grill for direct-heat cooking over high heat. Place a pizza stone suitable for use on an outdoor grill on the grill to preheat. Using a rolling pin, roll one portion of dough onto a work surface sprinkled with flour until you have a thin pizza base. Repeat with the remaining dough. Prick the bases all over with a fork to stop air bubbles from forming when cooking. Spread the tomato sauce over the pizza bases and sprinkle with the mozzarella, cherry tomatoes, parsley, olives, anchovies, capers, pepper flakes, garlic and torn pieces of buffalo mozzarella. Season lightly with salt and pepper.

Cook the pizzas for about 5–10 minutes or until golden and crispy. Drizzle with olive oil, top with basil leaves and serve.

NOTE: The pizza dough makes enough for four 12-inch pizzas. The tomato pizza sauce makes about 2 cupfuls (or enough for about 8 pizzas). It can be frozen.

4 ounces mozzarella cheese, shredded
1½ cups cherry tomatoes, sliced
1 large handful of fresh Italian parsley, chopped
24 olives, pitted and cut in half
12 white anchovy fillets
2 tablespoons capers, rinsed
pinch of red pepper flakes
1 garlic clove, finely chopped
1–2 balls of buffalo milk mozzarella cheese
olive oil, for drizzling
1 large handful of fresh basil leaves

PIZZA DOUGH
3 teaspoons active dry yeast
3 teaspoons sugar
3 teaspoons salt
1 tablespoon olive oil
2¾ cups bread flour, plus extra for dusting

TOMATO PIZZA SAUCE
1 can (14 ounces) tomatoes
pinch of black peppercorns
pinch of dried oregano

This is a variation on the recipe that won the best pizza award in Australia in 2008. The beauty of it lies in its simplicity, with just a few standout ingredients turning an ordinary pizza base into a standout dish for any lunch or dinner. These days you can buy pizza stones for your outdoor grill or you can cook this in a woodfired oven (or in a domestic pizza oven). Just take your pizza base and cover it with the tomato sauce and mascarpone mixture and bake it with the hood down on the grill until it is golden and crispy, then top it with the salmon and salad ingredients – perfect on a hot summer's day with a glass of chilled white wine.

salmon, mascarpone & caviar pizza

SERVES 4

1 batch of pizza dough
  (see recipe opposite)
8 ounces mascarpone cheese
3 ounces ricotta cheese
½ batch of tomato sauce
  (see recipe opposite)
4 ounces mozzarella
  cheese, shredded
1 large handful of fresh Italian
  parsley, chopped
¼ red onion, finely sliced
3 tablespoons light cream
zest of 1 lemon
12 slices smoked salmon
1 handful of fresh chives, snipped
1 handful of watercress leaves
2 tablespoons caviar
olive oil, for drizzling
4 lemon cheeks or halves
2 tablespoons capers, rinsed

Set up the outdoor grill for direct-heat cooking over high heat. Place a pizza stone suitable for use on an outdoor grill on the grill to preheat. Using a rolling pin, roll out one ball of dough onto a work surface sprinkled with flour until you have a thin pizza base. Repeat with the remaining dough. Prick the bases all over with a fork to stop air bubbles from forming when cooking.

Mix half of the mascarpone with the ricotta and spread over the pizza base, then spread the tomato sauce over the top. Sprinkle with the mozzarella, parsley and onion. Season lightly with salt and pepper.

Mix together the remaining mascarpone, cream and lemon zest and set aside.

Cook the pizzas for about 5–10 minutes, or until golden and crispy. Top with the smoked salmon, the mascarpone mixture, chives, watercress and caviar. Drizzle with olive oil and serve with a lemon cheek and sprinkle over the capers.

It was the move to Queensland's Gold Coast (where it's hot and sunny all year) from Melbourne as a boy that helped shape my love of the outdoors and especially the ocean. It was through this love of the outdoors that my appetite for food became apparent — after surfing nearly every day before and after school and the 30-minute bike ride there and back, I learned to crave lots of food – none more than mom's steak sandwich. It was a great thing to come home to after an evening out. Nothing fancy here: white bread, onions, cheese, good steak and iceberg lettuce (I have added the beet now but I hated it as a kid). You can jazz it up if you like but I think this version is still the best. Cheers, Mom.

mom's steak sandwich

SERVES 4

Set up the outdoor grill for direct-heat cooking over high heat. Place a griddle, *plancha* or *piastra* suitable for use on an outdoor grill on the grill to preheat. Toss the onion in a bowl with the rosemary and a little oil and cook on the griddle for about 8 minutes or until golden.

Season the steaks with salt and pepper and lightly coat in a little of the oil. Cook on the griddle for about 2 minutes each side or until medium-rare. Transfer to a platter. Top the steaks with the onions, then the cheese and let stand for 1–2 minutes.

Butter the bread and place onto the hot griddle to toast lightly.

Place four pieces of the toast on a work surface and top with the lettuce, steak, beet, sliced tomato and the condiments of choice. Top with the remaining toast slices, cut in half and serve.

1 onion, thickly sliced
pinch of chopped fresh rosemary
olive oil, for cooking
4 x 4-ounce sirloin steaks, pounded
   to flatten slightly
4 slices Cheddar cheese (or other
   cheese of your liking such as
   Swiss or provolone)
butter, for bread
8 slices white bread
4 large iceberg lettuce leaves
4 slices canned beet
1 vine-ripened tomato, thinly sliced
condiments, such as ketchup,
   barbecue sauce, mustard and
   mayonnaise, to serve

This is a really easy way of feeding a crowd at your next barbecue without going down the old sausage-in-bread-with-tomato-sauce route (even though I adore grilled sausages with tomato sauce in a bun). This recipe is a celebration of healthy ingredients: chicken, fresh herbs, yogurt and flatbread, all wrapped up like they do in the kebab shops. Except this version tastes better, and you don't need to wait until midnight to eat this (after too many drinks) — they actually taste awesome in the daytime, too.

chicken shawarma with yogurt & garlic sauce

SERVES 4

3 tablespoons lemon juice
pinch of salt
2 tablespoons olive oil
2 teaspoons ground allspice
1 tablespoon ground coriander
3 tablespoons chopped fresh
   cilantro leaves
2½ pounds boneless, skinless
   chicken thighs, fat trimmed
6 white flatbreads
2 large handfuls of shredded
   iceberg lettuce

YOGURT & GARLIC SAUCE
8 garlic cloves
2 teaspoons salt
3 tablespoons lemon juice
½ cup sunflower oil
¾ cup olive oil
½ cup plain yogurt
2 teaspoons sumac (see note)

TOMATO-PARSLEY SALAD
3 handfuls of fresh Italian
   parsley, chopped
1 vine-ripened tomato, diced
¼ small onion, thinly sliced

Set up the outdoor grill for direct-heat cooking over medium-high heat. Combine the lemon juice, salt, oil, spices, and cilantro in a large bowl. Add the chicken and toss to coat.

Cook the chicken on the grill for 4–5 minutes on each side, or until cooked through. Cut into bite-sized pieces.

Meanwhile, to make the yogurt and garlic sauce, blend the garlic, salt and lemon juice in a blender until smooth. Gradually add the oils in a thin steady stream while the motor is still running, until the sauce has thickened, then fold in the yogurt and sumac.

To make the salad, combine the parsley, tomato and onion.

To assemble, place the flatbreads on the grill for about 5–10 seconds to warm, then spread with the yogurt and garlic sauce. Arrange the tomato-parsley salad, lettuce and chicken on top. Roll up to enclose and cut in half to serve.

NOTE: Sumac is a lemony spice used in Middle Eastern cooking. Look for it in Middle Eastern markets or specialty food stores.

A quesadilla is a toasted tortilla that has been filled with cheese and folded (think of it as a Mexican grilled sandwich). I have made them here by sandwiching the filling between two tortillas instead of one as I think it is easier to do it this way. For another quick snack idea, simply fill with cheese and jalapeño peppers, but if you want something with a bit more substance fill with your favorite refried beans or chili con carne mixture and let the party begin.

chili bean quesadillas

SERVES 4

Heat the oil in a skillet over medium-high heat and cook the onion, garlic and green chile until softened. Add the cumin, paprika and chile powder and cook until fragrant. Stir in the tomatoes and ½ cup of water and mix well. Simmer for 15 minutes or until the sauce has reduced and is thick. Add the kidney beans and season with salt and pepper.

Set up the outdoor grill for direct-heat cooking over medium-high heat. Place a griddle, *plancha* or *piastra* suitable for use on an outdoor grill on the grill to preheat. Divide the chili bean mixture among 4 tortillas, then sprinkle with the cilantro, jalapeños and cheese and top each with another tortilla. Cook on the griddle with a touch of oil for a few minutes until golden, then flip over and and cook until golden on the other side. Cut into pieces and serve with sour cream and lime wedges.

2 tablespoons olive oil
1 large onion, chopped
2 garlic cloves, crushed
2 jalapeño chiles, seeded and chopped
1 tablespoon ground cumin
1 tablespoon paprika
pinch of pure chile powder
1 can (14 ounces) crushed tomatoes
1 can (14 ounces) red kidney beans, rinsed and drained
8 flour tortillas
3 tablespoons chopped fresh cilantro leaves
4 jalapeño chiles, sliced
1 cup shredded mozzarella cheese
8 tablespoons sour cream
lime wedges, to serve

I love to bring the wok down to the outdoor grill (I have a wok burner on the side of mine) and cook up some of my favorite things to eat, including crabs, of course. All types of crab are great cooked in this Asian sauce. The preparation is very simple to put together, you just need to shallow-fry the crabs first in batches, that way they cook evenly, then you can pop them all back in with the sauce and serve with a few cold beers. If you don't have a wok burner on your outdoor grill, it's best to cook this recipe in a wok on your stove inside. Heating oil outdoors over an open flame could be unsafe.

wok-fried crab with thai basil & eggplant

SERVES 2

3 live crabs
2 cups vegetable oil, for frying
1 cup tapioca flour (see note)
2 Asian eggplants, sliced into 2-inch pieces
1 large red serrano chile, sliced
2 garlic cloves, crushed
2 tablespoons Asian fish sauce
4 tablespoons oyster sauce
4 tablespoons kecap manis (sweet soy sauce)
1 cup vegetable broth
⅓ cup sliced bamboo shoots
1 large handful fresh Thai basil

Put the crabs in the freezer for about an hour until they are immobilized (but not frozen). Remove the gills (the spongy gray fingers) and any muck by rinsing very lightly and quickly under running water.

Using a cleaver, cut each crab into four pieces.

Heat 1¼ cups of the oil in a wok until hot. Meanwhile, toss the crab pieces with the flour in a large bowl, coating evenly.

When the oil is ready, carefully add the crab pieces to the wok four at a time and cook for 5 minutes. Remove and continue cooking the crab in batches. Allow the oil to cool, then carefully strain into a separate container and set aside.

Add the remaining oil to the wok and, when hot, stir-fry the eggplant until golden. Add the chile and garlic. Cook for another 1–2 minutes, then return the crab to the wok. Add the fish sauce, oyster sauce, kecap manis, vegetable broth and bamboo shoots, tossing as you go. When the sauce boils, the dish is ready to serve. Top with Thai basil and serve immediately.

NOTE: Look for tapioca flour in specialty food stores or natural foods stores.

I love the way Australia has embraced the foods from other nationalities with such conviction and with such open arms. In the Sydney suburb of Bondi where I live, we have Thai, Chinese, Vietnamese, Mexican, Russian, Portuguese, French, Italian, Indian, Japanese, Korean, Spanish, Lebanese and Turkish restaurants to name just a few. It's not only what we choose to go out and eat but what we stay home and cook for ourselves – long gone are the meat and three vegetables on a table every night. Now we cook up a quick stir-fry, a slow braised tagine or even a lovely curry. This recipe — perfectly balanced with the steak, fresh herbs and noodles — is a great one to cook on an outdoor grill and present to family and friends when they come over as it pleases everyone without being too filling.

thai beef salad

SERVES 4

Set up the outdoor grill for direct-heat cooking over high heat. Place a griddle, *plancha* or *piastra* suitable for use on an outdoor grill on the grill to preheat. Put the salt and pepper in a shallow dish and roll the beef in it evenly. Pour some olive oil onto the griddle and cook the beef for 4–5 minutes on each side until seared all over and rare inside. Let stand for 10 minutes before slicing (or place into the fridge and let cool before slicing).

Place the noodles in a heatproof bowl and pour over some boiling water. Set aside until tender, about 5–10 minutes. Rinse and drain.

To make the dressing, combine the ginger, cilantro, garlic, chile, sugar, vinegar, soy, lemongrass, sesame oil and olive oil in a bowl. Pour half of the dressing over the noodles.

To serve, place the noodles on a platter and top with the beef slices, then top with the herbs, remaining dressing and the peanuts and toss to combine. You can serve this dish at room temperature or cold.

3 tablespoons sea salt
3 tablespoons cracked black peppercorns
1¼ pounds filet mignon (1 long piece preferable)
olive oil, for cooking
4 ounces rice vermicelli noodles
3 green onions, thinly sliced on the diagonal
1 small handful of fresh Thai basil
1 small handful of fresh mint
1 small handful of fresh cilantro leaves
2 tablespoons chopped roasted peanuts

DRESSING
2 tablespoons finely chopped fresh ginger
2 tablespoons finely chopped fresh cilantro stems
3 garlic cloves, finely chopped
1 large red serrano chile, thinly sliced
1 tablespoon light brown sugar
2 tablespoons rice vinegar
2 tablespoons soy sauce
1 tablespoon finely chopped lemongrass stalk (white part only)
1 teaspoon sesame oil
3 tablespoons extra-virgin olive oil

The bloody Mary is one of those classic cocktails that most people know. Whether you add a hint of horseradish, basil or extra chile, this is one of my favorite cocktails — with or without vodka. The other great thing about the bloody Mary is that you can serve it first thing in the morning to cure a hangover, before lunch, or in the form of an oyster shot when guests arrive for a barbecue.

signature bloody mary

SERVES 4

To make the Mary mix, combine the Worcestershire sauce, Tabasco, salts, peppers and horseradish. Add a quarter of the mixture to a cocktail shaker along with a quarter each of the vodka, lemon juice and tomato juice. Stir to combine. Pour over ice into a glass and repeat with the remaining ingredients.

GLASS: Highball
GARNISH: Rub the edge of the empty glass with a lemon wedge and dip it into some cracked black pepper and coarse salt. Add a celery rib or basil leaves to serve.

8 ounces vodka (Absolut Peppar – a chile-flavored vodka – works well)
¼ cup lemon juice
1½ cups tomato juice

MARY MIX
1 tablespoon Worcestershire sauce
8 drops Tabasco sauce
3 pinches of celery salt
2 pinches of coarse salt
2 pinches each of ground white and black pepper
2 pinches of cayenne pepper
1½ teaspoon grated fresh horseradish root

I don't think there is a child who doesn't love raspberry lemonade, and there are some adults who love it just as much. This fancy-pants version, with the addition of lemon sherbet and fresh raspberries, will tempt most grown-ups.

raspberry lemonade mocktail

SERVES 4–6

Put the sherbet, raspberries, lemon juice and sugar syrup into a blender, blend and pour into glasses, then top with soda.

GLASS: Rocks or old-fashioned
GARNISH SUGGESTIONS: Grenadine float and raspberries.

4 scoops of lemon sherbet
18 fresh raspberries
2½ ounces lemon juice
1¼ ounces sugar syrup
  (see recipe p84)
1¼ ounces club soda

Sangria is the national drink of Spain and Portugal. Traditionally it's made with red wine, fruit, orange juice and a sweetener; however, there's a whole lot more to this drink than that. To give it a little more spice and kick, we've added some Cognac and extra herbs and spices. Serve it over ice with plenty of fruit.

sangria

SERVES 4–6

Add all the ingredients to a pitcher and allow to sit. Pour into glasses.

GLASS: Highball
GARNISH SUGGESTIONS: Fresh fruit, cinnamon stick and mint sprigs.

6 ounces dry red wine
2 ounces cognac
2 ounces orange juice
12 fresh raspberries
12 fresh blueberries
2 blood oranges, cut into wedges
1 ruby red grapefruit, cut
  into wedges
12 fresh mint leaves
2 cinnamon sticks
2 star anise

For the bourbon drinker, this is the drink to get you one step closer to drinking cocktails. All of the ingredients are easily found in most supermarkets. And if you want, you can add some glamour to the drink by adding blood orange or tangerine juice — this is sure to show the neighbors who is boss.

lynchburg lemonade
SERVES 4–6

6 ounces bourbon
2 ounces Cointreau
1¼ ounces lemon juice
1¼ ounces lime juice
2 ounces sugar syrup
   (see recipe p84)
2 ounces club soda

Add a quarter or a sixth of all the ingredients except the soda into a boston cocktail shaker, add ice, shake and strain over ice into a glass. Repeat with the remaining ingredients. Top with soda.

GLASS: Highball
GARNISH SUGGESTIONS: A lemon wedge and maraschino cherry

No matter what ingredients you put in the glass — raspberries also work really well — all you need to do to finish off the drink is turn a swizzle stick between your hands to stir the cocktail and blend the ingredients.

lychee swizzle
SERVES 4

8 ounces vodka
1¼ ounces lychee liqueur
2½ ounces lychee juice
2 ounces lemon juice
½ ounce ginger syrup
   (see note)
4 lemongrass stalks

Add a quarter of all the ingredients to a glass, add crushed ice, and use the bulb of lemongrass to "swizzle" the drink. Top with crushed ice and leave the lemongrass stem in the glass. Repeat with the remaining ingredients.

GLASS: Highball
GARNISH SUGGESTIONS: Half-peeled lychees
NOTE: To make ginger syrup, bring ½ cup sugar and ½ cup water to a boil with a 1½-inch piece of ginger, grated. Boil for 5 minutes, then strain and cool.

into the evening

I used to own a restaurant in Sydney's Bondi Beach called Hugos and when I had to describe it to people, I used to say that the atmosphere was one of casual sophistication. And that is what I wanted to do with this chapter of the book — to elevate the humble outdoor grill to one of casual sophistication, while keeping the recipes as achievable as in the previous chapters. Well, okay, I always like to throw in a couple that are geared more towards the "serious" home cook who likes a bit of a challenge. Enjoy these dishes with the cocktails I've suggested, or a good bottle of wine, and when the sun sets, feel the warm glow from the grill — and the admiration of your satisfied guests.

This, of course, is not a dish to cook on the grill, but I couldn't do an outdoor book without including fresh oysters. I've recently learned how to shuck an oyster and I wish I had picked it up much earlier. The difference between shucking your own oyster and buying one already opened is huge, mainly because when you shuck your own, the oyster in your hand is still alive. When you open the shell, the oyster should be completely covered by a juice, and this juice is very tasty. When you buy oysters already shucked, generally they have been washed and all the lovely juices have been washed away as well. And remember, next time you're at the fish market, learn how to shuck your own.

freshly shucked oysters with ruby grapefruit, mint & chile

SERVES 4

Peel and segment the grapefruit and cut into small pieces. Set aside in a bowl, keeping any juices that run off.

Warm the vinegar in a small saucepan, then dissolve the sugar into it and season with salt and pepper. Remove from heat, whisk in the olive oil, add the grapefruit and juice, and allow to cool. Stir in the mint and chile.

Top each oyster with a spoonful of sauce and serve over ice.

1 ruby grapefruit
3 tablespoons red wine vinegar
1 tablespoon sugar
½ cup extra-virgin olive oil
1 large handful of fresh mint, very thinly sliced
1 red serrano chile, seeded and finely chopped
24 oysters, freshly shucked

This is a typical Spanish tapas dish, but you could also serve it as a starter or light meal. If you're a bit funny about eating baby octopus, then use squid tentacles, sardines, or pretty much any other seafood. Have some aïoli and crusty bread on hand and don't forget the Spanish sherry.

baby octopus with smoked spanish paprika & sweet & sour peppers

SERVES 4

1⅓ pounds cleaned baby octopus
   or squid tentacles
½ cup extra-virgin olive oil
1 tablespoon smoked
   Spanish paprika
store-bought aïoli, to serve
crusty bread, to serve

SWEET & SOUR PEPPERS
2 red bell peppers
2 yellow bell peppers
½ cup extra-virgin olive oil
1 red onion, sliced
½ cup sherry vinegar
½ cup firmly packed light
   brown sugar
1 bay leaf
1 large handful of fresh
   Italian parsley

Mix the octopus with the olive oil and the paprika and set aside.

Set up the outdoor grill for direct-heat cooking over high heat. To make the sweet and sour peppers, preheat a heavy-bottomed nonreactive saucepan on the grill. Cut the peppers into strips and sauté in the pan with the olive oil and the onion. Add the vinegar, sugar and bay leaf, then cook slowly for 20 minutes. Allow to cool, then add the parsley.

Place a griddle, *plancha* or *piastra* suitable for use on an outdoor grill on the grill to preheat. Place the octopus on the griddle and cook for 2 minutes on each side. Season with salt and serve with the sweet and sour peppers, some aïoli and crusty bread.

There is something extremely enticing about anything cooked in a banana leaf on an outdoor grill or over hot coals. It's a bit like Christmas and having a wonderful present to unwrap. A perfect accompaniment would be some steamed rice and a crisp salad.

barramundi fillets in banana leaf with black bean & chile sambal

SERVES 4

Soak the banana leaves in water overnight so they won't burn on the outdoor grill.

Set up the outdoor grill for direct-heat cooking over medium-high heat. Place a griddle, *plancha* or *piastra* suitable for use on an outdoor grill on the grill to preheat. Place the banana leaves on the griddle and heat until bright green, remove from heat and allow to cool. In a bowl, combine the sambal oelek, black beans and oyster sauce. Crisscross 2 banana leaves on a work surface and place a piece of fish in the center, then top with a couple of spoonfuls of the sauce mixture. Bring the 4 sides of the banana leaf up to form the parcel and secure with a toothpick.

Cook on the griddle with the lid down for 5 minutes, depending on the thickness of your fish, or until cooked through.

NOTE: Sambal oelek is an Indonesian chile paste, available from Asian markets.

Heating banana leaves makes them malleable and easy to fold. If banana leaves are unavailable, use aluminum foil.

16 banana leaves (see note)
2 tablespoons sambal oelek (see note)
½ cup canned salted black beans, rinsed and drained
4 tablespoons oyster sauce
4 x 6-ounce barramundi or sea bass fillets, skinned and cut in half

It's nice to make something a little out of the ordinary, especially when it's this easy. Try using wild kingfish steaks if you can as you get some of the belly which is my favorite part of this fish. You could also use salmon for this and, alternatively, you could serve the fish as a whole portion rather than flaking it. The crispy garlic and almonds add a great texture.

fish with crispy garlic & almond salad

SERVES 4

To make the Japanese dressing, combine all the ingredients in a nonreactive bowl and set aside.

Heat a little peanut oil in a skillet over medium-high heat. Add the garlic and cook for a few minutes or until golden and crispy. Remove and drain on paper towels.

Set up the outdoor grill for direct-heat cooking over medium-high heat. Coat the fish fillets with a little more of the oil. Season with salt and pepper and place, skin side down, on the grill. Cook for a few minutes until golden, then turn over and cook for another 1–2 minutes or until just cooked through.

In a bowl combine the arugula, mizuna, frisée, mint and cilantro, leek and chile and pour over the salad dressing. Toss to combine.

Flake the fish over the salad, discarding the bones if using steaks, and serve scattered with the crispy garlic and almonds.

1 tablespoon peanut oil
6 garlic cloves, thinly sliced
4 x 6-ounce white-fleshed fish
    fillets or steaks
2 large handfuls of baby arugula
2 large handfuls of baby
    mizuna leaves
2 large handfuls of frisée
    lettuce leaves
1 small handful of fresh mint
1 handful of fresh cilantro leaves
3 tablespoons julienned leek
1 banana chile, cut into thin strips
4 tablespoons toasted
    chopped almonds

JAPANESE SALAD DRESSING
½ cup grapeseed oil
⅓ cup Japanese rice vinegar
2 teaspoons sliced green onion,
    white part only
2 teaspoons English mustard
2 teaspoons light soy sauce
2 teaspoons mirin (Japanese
    cooking wine)
few drops of Asian fish sauce
pinch of pure chile powder

The sauce in this dish is simply to die for. It works with all types of seafood but my favorite is the delicate flesh of the freshwater crayfish. Think of them as a small lobsters. I'm an olive oil-man myself, but the butter in this makes it spectacular.

grilled crayfish with thyme, sambuca & orange butter

SERVES 4

To make the thyme, sambuca and orange butter, place the orange juice in a saucepan over medium-high heat. Bring to a boil and simmer until reduced to about 2½ tablespoons. Set aside to cool completely. Then add the butter, zest, lemon juice, thyme, chervil, fennel and sambuca and gently melt over low heat, stirring to combine. Process in a food processor until blended, then season with salt and pepper. Roll the butter in plastic wrap to form a cylinder and refrigerate until set.

Put the crayfish in the freezer for ½ hour until they are immobilized (but not frozen). Split the crayfish down the center with a sharp, heavy knife and remove the entrails.

Set up the outdoor grill for direct-heat cooking over high heat. Place a griddle, *plancha* or *piastra* suitable for use on an outdoor grill on the grill to preheat. Cook the lemon and the crayfish on the griddle, placing the crayfish flesh side down, for a couple of minutes until the flesh of the crayfish is just opaque and cooked through. Serve the crayfish with the lemon, topped with a thin slice of the thyme, sambuca and orange butter.

NOTE: Depending on what part of the country you live in, you may need to special-order the crayfish from your fishmonger.

8 large crayfish or small spiny lobsters
1 lemon, cut into wedges or halves

**THYME, SAMBUCA &
ORANGE BUTTER**
2 cups orange juice
1 cup unsalted butter, chopped
finely grated zest of 1 orange
juice of 2 lemons
½ bunch of fresh lemon thyme, chopped
1 bunch of fresh chervil, chopped
1 teaspoon ground fennel
3 tablespoons white sambuca

I can remember making this recipe as a special at my restaurant Hugos Bondi close to 15 years ago with Simon Fawcett, my head chef at the time. He was a wonderful inspiration for me in the kitchen as he used to get very excited over the way flavors worked. He made up this dressing using ketchup and I thought he was joking — we were an award-winning restaurant! Well, I was so pleasantly surprised at how good it tasted when mixed with the fish and salad that I changed my mind and it ended up on the menu for that summer. I often make this sauce and team it with anything from seafood to sausages.

grilled salmon with cucumber spaghetti & tomato-herb dressing

SERVES 4

16 baby beets
2 long cucumbers, washed
    and put through a mandoline
    or cut into long thin strips
    that resemble spaghetti
1 cup orange juice
¼ cup Pernod
4 x 6-ounce Atlantic salmon
    fillets, skin on
olive oil, for cooking

TOMATO-HERB DRESSING
2 shallots, finely diced
2 tablespoons finely chopped
    fresh chives
2 tablespoons chopped fresh parsley
1 tablespoon finely chopped
    fresh chervil
1 cup extra-virgin olive oil
3 tablespoons red wine vinegar
    or sherry vinegar
scant ½ cup ketchup
a few drops of Tabasco sauce
splash of Worcestershire sauce

Set up the outdoor grill for direct-heat cooking over medium-high heat. Wrap the beets in aluminum foil and cook on the grill until tender, about 20 minutes. Cool and peel.

To make the cucumber spaghetti, combine the cucumber, orange juice, Pernod and a pinch of salt and let stand for 20 minutes, then drain.

To make the dressing, mix together the shallots, herbs, olive oil, vinegar, ketchup, Tabasco and Worcestershire sauces and season with salt and pepper.

Place a griddle, *plancha* or *piastra* suitable for use on an outdoor grill on the grill to preheat. Brush the salmon with a little oil and place on the griddle, skin side down, for 4 minutes or until crisp and golden, then turn and cook for another 3 minutes. Remove and let rest for a few minutes for medium-rare.

Toss the beets with a touch of oil and grill for 1–2 minutes to heat through. Divide the cucumber spaghetti among 4 plates, spoon the dressing around the plate, and top with the salmon and the beets.

This is a very quick recipe once you have assembled all the ingredients. It is fiery hot with a smoky flavor — be cautious when using it and have a cold beer on hand!

scallops grilled in the shell with chipotle chile & cilantro butter

SERVES 4 AS ENTRÉE

Set up the outdoor grill for direct-heat cooking over medium heat. Place a griddle, *plancha* or *piastra* suitable for use on an outdoor grill on the grill to preheat. To prepare the scallops, make sure they are free of any grit and the muscle on the side of the scallop is removed.

To make the topping, combine the butter with the cilantro, lime juice, garlic and chipotle chile in a bowl and mix until well blended. Place 2 teaspoons of butter on each scallop and season with salt and pepper.

Place the shells on the griddle and cook for 4–5 minutes with the lid closed until the butter is sizzling and the scallops are just cooked.

NOTE: Ask your fishmonger for scallops in the shell. If you cannot find them, place the scallops and the sauce on folded banana leaves instead.

20 scallops on the half shell
1 cup butter, at room temperature
1 large handful of fresh cilantro leaves, finely chopped
juice of 4 limes
2 garlic cloves, crushed
1 tablespoon chipotle chiles in adobo sauce

Clams, mussels and cockles all make for wonderful eating — they're not too expensive and are the perfect fingerfood to serve at an informal outdoor grill. They're also quite interesting to eat as they aren't the norm. The gorgeous thing about a dish like this is that it is all packaged in aluminum foil, then plonked onto the grill and left to cook for 10 minutes or so while you are catching up on all the gossip or telling some tall tales about the one that got away.

clams with sweet corn, jalapeño & cilantro salsa

SERVES 4

Soak the clams in cold water overnight in the refrigerator to remove any grit.

Set up the outdoor grill for direct-heat cooking over medium heat. To prepare the salsa, peel the corn, brush with a little oil and grill, turning occasionally, for 15–20 minutes or until tender. Remove the kernels by cutting down the sides of the cob.

Add more coals to the fire bed or increase the heat to high. Cook the bell pepper on the hot grill, turning occasionally, for 15–20 minutes or until the skin turns black. Remove from the grill and set aside until cool. Wipe away the skin leaving the flesh. Cut in half, seed and finely dice.

Combine the corn, pepper, chopped onion, jalapeño chiles and cilantro in a bowl. Add the lime juice, tequila and olive oil and season with salt and pepper.

Take 8 large sheets of heavy-duty aluminum foil and lay 2 on top of each other. Place a quarter of the clams in the center of one foil square. Pour a quarter of the salsa mixture over the clams, seal the foil into a package and seal all the way around leaving no gaps. Repeat with the remaining ingredients and foil. Place the parcels on the grill and cook for 10 minutes or until all the clams are open. Serve with crusty bread to soak up the delicious juices.

4½ pounds clams
4 ears corn
1 red bell pepper
1 red onion, finely chopped
2 jalapeño chiles, chopped
1 large handful of fresh
  cilantro leaves
juice of 8 limes
½ cup tequila
1 cup extra-virgin olive oil
crusty bread, to serve

If you're looking for something to really impress, then look no further than the highly revered spot prawns. We catch a similar species off the coast of Western Australia and New Zealand, where they are snap-frozen on the boats, then boxed up and sent around the globe. You could quite easily substitute large shrimp in their place if you can't find spot prawns. The best way to serve them is grilled with a touch of garlic and herb butter, but for something a bit more out of the ordinary and very impressive, try this simple dressing using young coconut, mango and lime.

grilled spot prawns with mango, young coconut & lime

SERVES 4

2 young coconuts
2 mangoes
½ cup coconut cream
1 long green chile, seeded and
   finely chopped
juice of 4 limes
1 tablespoon Asian fish sauce
6 green onions, sliced
20 spot prawns

Ask your grocer to cut open your young coconut or, if you have a cleaver at home, you can do it yourself. Using a spoon, scoop out the soft flesh from the inside and dice.

Peel and finely dice the mangoes and put in a large bowl. Add the coconut flesh, coconut cream, chile, lime juice, fish sauce and green onions.

Set up the outdoor grill for direct-heat cooking over medium heat. Place a griddle, *plancha* or *piastra* suitable for use on an outdoor grill on the grill to preheat.

Cut the spot prawns in half lengthwise and remove the vein. Season with salt and pepper and cook on the griddle for a couple of minutes until opaque and just cooked through. Serve drizzled with the mango dressing.

NOTE: Look for young coconut and unsweetened coconut cream in Asian food markets. Do not substitute with sweetened cream of coconut.

This is a taste of the Greek islands. If you have not tried fresh sardines before, you are in for a treat — they are a million miles away from the canned variety and very affordable.

sardines in grape leaves with cherry tomatoes & olives

SERVES 4

1 bunch of fresh oregano

12 whole fresh sardines

12 marinated grape leaves, rinsed

2 anchovy fillets

1 garlic clove, crushed

1 tablespoon finely sliced preserved lemon peel

1 handful of fresh Italian parsley, chopped

1 cup cherry tomatoes, cut into halves

½ cup kalamata olives, pitted

juice of 2 lemons

⅔ cup extra-virgin olive oil

olive oil, for cooking

Place a sprig of oregano inside each sardine, then wrap in a grape leaf. Season with salt and pepper.

To make the dressing, crush the anchovies in a bowl with a fork. Chop the remaining oregano leaves and add to the anchovies along with the garlic, preserved lemon, parsley, tomatoes, olives, lemon juice and oil.

Set up the outdoor grill for direct-heat cooking over medium heat. Brush the sardines with a little oil, then grill for 4 minutes on each side, or until cooked through. Serve 3 sardines per person, topped with the dressing.

This is a style of food I so love to eat and also cook – a beautiful piece of fish that you have either caught or bought, married with a light flavorful salsa that only takes a matter of minutes to put together. And the best thing of all is that you know you are doing yourself and your guests a favor by cooking it as it's delicious and healthy.

grilled fish with an italian garden salsa of artichokes & tomato

SERVES 4

To make the salsa, cut the tomatoes into quarters and discard the seeds. Finely dice the tomato flesh and artichokes and place in a bowl. Add the olives, parsley and pine nuts, then add the oil and lemon juice, and season with salt and pepper.

Set up the outdoor grill for direct-heat cooking over high heat. Place a griddle, *plancha* or *piastra* suitable for use on an outdoor grill on the grill to preheat. Brush the fish with some oil and cook on the griddle for a few minutes on each side, or until cooked through, depending on how thick the fish is. Serve with the salsa.

4 vine-ripened tomatoes
1 jar (5½ ounces) marinated artichokes, drained
1 cup pitted kalamata olives
1 handful of fresh Italian parsley, chopped
¼ cup pine nuts, toasted
⅔ cup extra-virgin olive oil
juice of 1 lemon
4 x 6-ounce pieces of fish such as snapper, sea bass or halibut
olive oil, for cooking

Chicken and corn is such a great combination — think of chicken and corn soup. This is why this recipe is great as it combines those two ingredients into a grown-up dish. Of course, you could chop up the chicken and mix it with the risotto, but I think by grilling the chicken and serving it with the risotto, you get a better flavor and presentation. This is a great meal to serve when the weather is a bit on the cool side.

grilled chicken breast with shallots & corn risotto

SERVES 4

8 shallots
4 boneless chicken breast
 halves, skin on
2 tablespoons olive oil
baby arugula, to serve

SWEET ONION BUTTER
1 red onion, finely chopped
olive oil, for cooking
1 tablespoon light brown sugar
1 cup butter, softened
2 tablespoons chopped fresh chives

CORN RISOTTO
2 garlic cloves, crushed
olive oil, for cooking
2 teaspoons fresh thyme leaves
1 cup corn kernels (either off
 the cob or canned)
2/3 cup Arborio rice
1/2 cup dry white wine
1 1/4 cups hot chicken broth, plus
 more if needed

Set up the outdoor grill for direct-heat cooking over medium heat. To make the sweet onion butter, sauté the onion in a skillet on the grill in a touch of oil until soft, then add the sugar and cook until caramelized. Mix the butter with the onion and chives until melted. Season well with salt and pepper. Remove from the heat and set aside.

Wrap the shallots in aluminum foil and cook on the grill for 30 minutes or until softened. Take the shallots out of the foil. Set aside.

Rub the chicken breasts with olive oil and place them, skin side down, on the grill. Cook for about 7 minutes, or until the skin is golden, then turn over and cook for another 4–5 minutes. Set aside to rest for 5 minutes, then slice.

Meanwhile, make your risotto in a saucepan on the side burner or stove top by frying the garlic in a little oil over medium-low heat. Add the thyme and corn and cook for 1 minute, then add the rice and cook for another minute, stirring so the grains are all coated with the oil. Add the wine and cook for another minute, stirring, then add all the broth. Stir once, cover with the lid and reduce the heat to low. Check it in about 12 minutes — if it's too dry, and the rice is still a little firm, add a bit more hot broth.

Serve the risotto topped with the shallots and chicken, drizzled with the sweet onion butter and topped with some baby arugula.

The best way to speed up cooking meat on the grill is to butterfly it so that it cooks in half the time. I wouldn't recommend doing this every time because you end up with less room for error in the way you want it cooked, as the thicker the piece of meat, the more control you have over the doneness. But in this case, butterflied is the way to go — not only is it super-quick to cook, it also works so well with the simple arugula salad that it's teamed with.

butterflied lamb loin with arugula salad

SERVES 4

Place the garlic, chile, rosemary and half the extra-virgin olive oil on a baking sheet. Season well with sea salt and cracked black pepper and coat the lamb in the mixture.

Set up the outdoor grill for direct-heat cooking over high heat. Place the lamb on the grill and cook for a few minutes on each side or until pink in the center. Let rest for a few minutes.

Combine the arugula with the vinegar and remaining olive oil and toss with some sea salt and cracked black pepper, and top with the ricotta.

Serve the lamb with the arugula salad and lemon wedges.

2 garlic cloves, finely chopped
1 red Thai chile, finely chopped
1 tablespoon chopped fresh rosemary
3 tablespoons extra-virgin olive oil
4 x 6-ounce lamb loin, butterflied lengthwise
6 cups baby arugula
2 tablespoons aged balsamic vinegar
4 tablespoons ricotta cheese
lemon wedges, to serve

Anthony Ross, executive chef at the Langham Hotel in Melbourne, once took me on a tour of the kitchen. The food there is amazing and so I asked Anthony for his recipe for pork belly tandoori as it is my favorite. He said it was quite funny because in India pork isn't really seen as a popular choice for tandoori, but in Australia it is his bestseller. I have changed the pork belly to loin as it suits the grill better.

tandoori pork on the outdoor grill

SERVES 4

14-ounce pork loin or tenderloin
naan bread, to serve
plain yogurt, to serve
1 small cucumber, julienned

MARINADE
2 x 4-inch pieces of fresh ginger,
    peeled and finely chopped
12 garlic cloves, finely chopped
1 tablespoon ground cumin
1 tablespoon ground coriander
1 tablespoon sweet paprika
2½ teaspoons garam masala
1 teaspoon ground fenugreek
2 teaspoons Indian chile paste
    (see note)
5 tablespoons lemon juice
¼ cup mustard oil
    (see note)

Soak 8 wooden skewers in water overnight.

To make the marinade, combine all the ingredients in a nonreactive bowl.

Cut the pork into 1-inch cubes. Add the pork to the marinade, toss to coat and refrigerate for at least 3 hours.

Set up the outdoor grill for direct-heat cooking over high heat. Thread the pork onto the skewers (use gloves to avoid staining your hands) and cook on the grill for 5 minutes on each side or until cooked through. Warm the naan bread briefly on the grill and serve with the tandoori pork, yogurt and cucumber.

NOTE: Fenugreek, Indian chile paste and mustard oil are available from Indian grocery stores or large Asian markets.

When I got my first job in television, I was discussing with the bosses there the type of show they wanted to make. I was a bit nervous about what where they going to ask of me in a culinary way as I was still defining my own style within my restaurants. I needn't have worried because they let me have free reign for five years. However, there was one stipulation: "Pete, you can do whatever you want, just no bloody seared tuna salads." I promised them I wouldn't do one on the show and I stayed true to my word. Many years later and with a grill cookbook to write, I think it is time to include one.

seared tuna with seaweed and ponzu salad

SERVES 4

Set up the outdoor grill for direct-heat cooking over high heat. Place a griddle, *plancha* or *piastra* suitable for use on an outdoor grill on the grill to preheat. Dry-toast the Szechuan and black peppercorns and salt in a small frying pan on the grill for a few minutes or until fragrant. Grind in a mortar and pestle until fine, then set aside.

To make the dressing, blend the yolks, whole egg and ponzu with a blender. With the motor still running, slowly add the oil to form a texture like mayonnaise. Add the reserved cucumber juice and lime juice and season with salt and pepper.

In a bowl, mix the seaweed, cucumber, daikon and chile together with some of the dressing.

Roll the tuna pieces in the toasted spices and sear on the griddle for 2 minutes on each side. Cut the tuna into pieces and top with the salad and fish roe. Serve the remaining dressing on the side.

NOTE: Ponzu is a Japanese soy, citrus and vinegar dressing and is available from Japanese markets. Wakame can also be found in Japanese markets. This dressing uses raw eggs. If you have health and safety concerns, do not consume raw eggs.

1 tablespoon Szechuan peppercorns
1 tablespoon black peppercorns
1 tablespoon sea salt
8 tablespoons fresh wakame seaweed (see note)
1 long cucumber, cut into ribbons using a vegetable peeler, juice saved for dressing (recipe below)
1 cup daikon, julienned
1 red serrano chile, cut into thin strips
4 x 4-ounce pieces tuna, either yellowfin or blue fin
1 tablespoon flying fish roe

TANGY PONZU DRESSING
2 egg yolks, plus 1 whole egg (see note)
scant ½ cup ponzu (see note)
1¾ cups vegetable oil
scant ½ cup reserved cucumber juice
juice of 1 lime

This is a wonderful recipe using calf's liver that has been cooked on the grill, then teamed with a lovely salad. I prefer the liver to be sliced thinly so it cooks very quickly and is more palatable. The liver has a very rich flavor but the vinegar cuts through it giving this dish a nice balance. Also, the longer you leave the onions in the dressing the better as the dressing will turn the onions bright pink, adding to the visual appeal of the dish.

grilled calf's liver with fig salad & sherry vinaigrette

SERVES 4

Set up the outdoor grill for direct-heat cooking over medium heat. Prepare the frisée by cutting at the base and removing the darker outer leaves — only use the lighter center ones for this dish.

Cook the pancetta on the stove top until crisp.

To make the dressing, gently cook the onion with a little oil in a small saucepan over low heat for 5 minutes until soft. Add the vinegar and let cool. Transfer to a bowl and whisk in the mustard, then the oils.

Season the calf's liver with salt and pepper and cook on the grill until pink, about 3—4 minutes on each side. Toss the frisée, pancetta and walnuts in a large bowl with some of the dressing and serve with the figs and liver.

1 head frisée lettuce
½ pound pancetta, thinly sliced
4 x 6-ounce calf's liver steaks
1 cup walnuts, toasted
6 fresh figs, quartered

SHERRY VINAIGRETTE
1 red onion, chopped
olive oil, for cooking
½ cup sherry vinegar
1 tablespoon Dijon mustard
½ cup walnut oil
1 cup peanut oil

This is a recipe we served when we first opened Hugos Manly in Sydney and it was designed by my head chef Leandro Panza. We had a couple of fish dishes on the menu that were beautiful and simple but I also wanted a dish on the menu that had a wow factor to it — this is it and it is very easy to make with no stress involved. The best part of this dish is the eggplant, it's a recipe that Leandro's mother taught him years ago, and it complements the grilled fish wonderfully.

snapper with marinated eggplant & truffle sauce

SERVES 4

Take the top off the eggplant and cut it in half lengthwise, then into three pieces. Season with salt, place in a steamer over a pot of boiling water, cover and cook for about 15 minutes until soft.

Combine the dried oregano, olive oil and red wine vinegar in a nonreactive bowl. Add the eggplant, let marinate for 5 minutes, then turn over and set aside.

Place the potatoes in a saucepan with cold water to cover and bring to a boil with a pinch of salt. Cook until tender, then let cool and toss with the basil oil.

To make the truffle dressing, combine the balsamic vinegar with the lemon juice and season with salt and pepper. Add the oils and egg yolk and whisk together until creamy.

Set up the outdoor grill for direct-heat cooking over medium-high heat. Season the snapper with salt and pepper and brush with a little olive oil, then cook on the grill for a few minutes on each side or until cooked through.

Serve the eggplant and basil potatoes topped with the snapper, drizzle over the truffle dressing and sprinkle with the chopped chives.

NOTE: This dressing contains raw eggs. If you have health and safety concerns, do not consume raw eggs.

2 eggplants
2 teaspoons dry oregano
½ cup extra-virgin olive oil
¼ cup aged red wine vinegar
2 potatoes, peeled and cut into ¾-inch cubes
1 tablespoon basil oil or pesto (see recipe p219)
4 x 6-ounce wild yellowtail snapper steaks or any other type of fish
3 tablespoons finely chopped fresh chives

TRUFFLE DRESSING
¼ cup white balsamic vinegar
1 teaspoon lemon juice
½ cup vegetable oil
2 teaspoons truffle oil
1 tablespoon extra-virgin olive oil
1 egg yolk (see note)

I remember absolutely hating anything to do with offal as a kid. I thought someone must be playing a cruel practical joke on me the first time I was served up lamb's liver by my dad... Well, I tried one mouthful and that put me off all things offaly until I was in my early 20s. I remember the first thing I tried was pâté and I adored it (it is still one of my favorite foods) and I thought if pâté is made from chicken or duck livers, then I had better try the real thing, simply cooked in a pan with a lovely sauce.

chicken livers with madeira, speck & potato galettes

SERVES 4

2 large potatoes, peeled
   and very thinly sliced
4 tablespoons clarified butter
   or ghee (see recipe p17)
2 shallots, chopped
⅓ pound speck, sliced (see note)
1 tablespoon olive oil
8 ounces chicken livers
4 tablespoons red wine vinegar
4 tablespoons Madeira
½ cup veal demiglace
   (see note)
1 small handful of fresh tarragon
1½ tablespoons butter
1 handful radicchio leaves, torn

To make the potato galettes, cut out circles of potato using a round cookie cutter about 2½ inches in diameter. Arrange the potatoes overlapping each other slightly to make 4 circles about 4 inches in diameter, and brush with clarified butter.

Set up the outdoor grill for direct-heat cooking over medium heat. Place a griddle, *plancha* or *piastra* suitable for use on an outdoor grill on the grill to preheat. Grease the griddle with 2 teaspoons of clarified butter, place the potato rings on the griddle and cook until golden. Turn over and continue cooking until golden on the other side. Remove and sprinkle with sea salt.

In a hot skillet on the grill, sauté the shallots and speck in the olive oil. Add the livers and cook until golden on one side, then turn over and deglaze with red wine vinegar and cook for 10 seconds. Add the Madeira and cook for another minute. Stir in the demiglace, tarragon and butter. Season to taste with salt and pepper. Sit for about 1 minute, then toss with the radicchio leaves.

Divide the livers among plates with the sauce and serve topped with the potato galettes.

NOTE: Veal demiglace is a reduction of veal stock available from specialty food stores and some butchers. If unavailable, substitute 1 cup rich veal or beef stock, reduced by half. Speck is a pork product similar to prosciutto, which is flavored with juniper. Look for it in specialty food stores or high-quality delicatessens

What a winner a dish like this is — super-easy, interesting, not expensive, and what a delight to prepare, cook and eat. This is what a grilled dinner is all about.

calamari with grilled fennel & charred lemon dressing

SERVES 4

1¼ pounds fresh baby calamari, cleaned, cut in half and scored on the inside

SALAD
1 large bulb of fennel, thinly sliced
½ cup olive oil
2 lemons
2 red serrano chiles, seeded and finely chopped
2 red onions, thinly sliced
1 handful of fresh mint
1 handful of fresh Italian parsley
1 cup lemon-infused extra-virgin olive oil

Set up the outdoor grill for direct-heat cooking over medium-high heat. Place a griddle, *plancha* or *piastra* suitable for use on an outdoor grill on the grill to preheat. To make the salad, toss the fennel with olive oil and place on the griddle. Cook until golden on one side, then turn and cook for another 2 minutes on the other side.

Finely grate the lemon zest and add the zest, chiles, onions and herbs to the fennel mixture. Cut the lemons in half. Cook the lemon halves on the griddle for 5 minutes. Remove and squeeze the juice over the salad. Add the lemon oil and season with salt and pepper.

Cook the calamari on the griddle for 1 minute or so on each side. Toss with the salad and serve immediately.

As you may be aware by now, I have two great culinary loves, Japanese food and grills, and I see no reason why the two should not live harmoniously in this book. This recipe is based on a dish I have eaten at many Japanese restaurants over the years and it is one I never tire of. Tataki of beef is a very briefly seared piece of meat that is then sliced and dressed with a lovely sauce. This recipe calls for the inclusion of crispy garlic chips which really makes the dish. I believe a great dish needs three things — the first is taste and flavor, the second is eye appeal (how good it looks) and the third is texture, which in this case is provided by the crispy garlic.

japanese beef tataki

SERVES 4

Set up the outdoor grill for direct-heat cooking over medium heat. Place a griddle, *plancha* or *piastra* suitable for use on an outdoor grill on the grill to preheat. Trim the filet of fat, then lightly brush with some olive oil and season with salt and pepper. Prepare an ice bath. Sear the beef on the griddle. Once colored well on all surfaces, plunge into the ice bath and allow to cool for about 3–4 minutes. Remove and drain well. Slice the beef tataki into thin slices and arrange on plates.

To make the onion ponzu, combine all the ingredients in a bowl.

To make the tataki dressing, combine all the ingredients in a bowl.

Slice the green onions as finely as possible into little circles and wash under running water for a few minutes, then drain and refrigerate.

Thinly slice the garlic, then heat ¾ inches of oil in a small deep saucepan over medium-high heat. Add the garlic and fry until golden and crispy. Remove with a slotted spoon. Drain on paper towels.

Drizzle the onion ponzu on top of the beef, then drizzle on some tataki dressing and top with the green onions, chives and crispy garlic.

¾ pound filet mignon
olive oil, for cooking
2 green onions
4 garlic cloves
1 tablespoon chopped fresh chives

ONION PONZU
1 white onion, very finely diced
   (as small as possible)
¼ teaspoon very finely chopped
   garlic (as small as possible)
3 tablespoons grapeseed oil
1 tablespoon lemon juice
1 tablespoon rice vinegar
1 tablespoon dark soy sauce
¼ teaspoon finely chopped
   fresh ginger

TATAKI DRESSING
5 tablespoons soy sauce
8 tablespoons rice vinegar
pinch of bonito flakes (optional)

I think this is one of the simplest and tastiest recipes I have ever come across. I had this on the menu at my restaurant Hugos Bondi in Sydney for 10 years and it was the most popular item on the menu, which was fantastic for me and my chefs as it was the easiest of all the dishes to cook. Just make sure when you are preparing this recipe that the avocados are ripe and the shrimp are fresh. For an even easier version, just buy cooked shrimp, peel them and pop them on top of the avocado.

shrimp & avocado stack

SERVES 4

1 red bell pepper
2 avocados, diced
1 plum tomato, seeded
    and chopped
1 Thai chile, finely chopped
1 tablespoon lemon juice, plus
    a little extra
1 tablespoon chopped fresh
    cilantro leaves
1 tablespoon extra-virgin olive oil
2 teaspoons diced red onion
4 teaspoons chile oil
16 raw medium shrimp, peeled,
    deveined, tails left intact
2 tablespoons olive oil
2 garlic cloves, chopped

BASIL OIL
1 handful fresh basil leaves
½ cup olive oil

To make the basil oil, blanch the basil in boiling water and refresh in ice water. Strain the water off and wring out the basil in a clean dish cloth to remove all moisture. Blend with the oil in a blender and season to taste with salt and pepper.

Set up the outdoor grill for direct-heat cooking over medium heat. Cook the bell pepper on the grill, turning occasionally, for about 15–20 minutes or until the skin turns black. Remove from the grill and let cool. Peel, seed, then finely dice.

Mix the avocado, tomato, bell pepper, chile, lemon juice, cilantro, olive oil, onion and sea salt and cracked pepper to taste in a bowl. Place a large round cookie cutter on a serving plate. Divide the avocado mixture into 4 portions and place one in the cookie cutter. Remove the cutter. Repeat 3 more times. Drizzle some of the basil and chile oils around each plate.

Place a griddle, *plancha* or *piastra* suitable for use on an outdoor grill on the grill to preheat. Season the shrimp with sea salt and black pepper and cook on the griddle until golden on one side, about 2 minutes, then turn over and cook on the other side until almost done, about 1 minute. Add the olive oil, garlic and extra lemon juice. Place the shrimp onto the avocado stacks and serve immediately.

Wagyu steak comes from a rare breed of cattle that has its bloodline traced back to Japan. The amazing thing about the cattle is that it has an increased amount of intermuscular marbling or fat than that of regular breeds of cattle, and this marbling brings a whole new level of flavor to the meat. This is a luxury item and I buy it only once or twice a year for special occasions. The rest of the time I just use a nice aged grass-fed piece of meat.

wagyu steak with mushrooms, potatoes and wild arugula

SERVES 4

4 shallots, peeled

4 x 8-ounce wagyu sirloin steaks

1 cup sliced fresh porcini mushrooms or other type of mushrooms

¾ pound fingerling potatoes, boiled until tender, peeled and sliced

olive oil, for cooking

1 garlic clove, finely chopped

⅔ cup veal demiglace (see note)

3 tablespoons extra-virgin olive oil

1 tablespoon balsamic vinegar

2 large handfuls of wild arugula

Set up the outdoor grill for direct-heat cooking over medium heat. Wrap the shallots in aluminum foil and cook on the edge of the grill where it is cooler for 30 minutes or until soft. Set aside to cool slightly, then cut into quarters.

Place a griddle, *plancha* or *piastra* suitable for use on an outdoor grill on the grill to preheat. Season each steak with salt and pepper and cook on the greased griddle for about 5 minutes, then turn over and cook for another 4 minutes. Let rest for 5 minutes in a warm place.

Meanwhile, place the mushrooms and potatoes on the griddle, drizzle with some oil and season with salt and pepper. Cook until golden on both sides, about 10 minutes, then add the garlic and cook for another minute. Heat the demiglace in a small saucepan over medium heat.

Place the potatoes, mushrooms and shallots on serving plates, then slice the meat and place on top. Pour over the demiglace.

In a bowl, mix together the olive oil and balsamic vinegar. Toss with the arugula, place onto the steak and serve immediately.

NOTE: Veal demiglace is a reduction of veal stock available from specialty food stores and some butchers. If unavailable, substitute 1 cup rich veal or beef stock, reduced by half.

I think chimichurri sauce is absolutely delicious and also makes the best marinade so I couldn't very well write a grill cookery book without including a recipe for it, could I? It's the South American take on pesto, only better.

t-bone steak with chimichurri sauce

SERVES 4

To make the sauce, first crush the garlic with a little salt in a mortar and pestle, or you could use a blender. Add the chile, parsley and cilantro leaves and pound or blend to a paste. Add the vinegar and cumin, then the olive oil and season with sea salt and cracked black pepper to taste.

Set up the outdoor grill for direct-heat cooking over medium-high heat. Oil the grill grate. Season the steaks with salt and pepper and cook for 6–7 minutes each side or until done to your liking. Remove from the heat and let rest in a warm place for 5 minutes, then serve with the sauce on top or on the side.

NOTE: You can make this dish indoors using a cast-iron skillet.

4 T-bone steaks, about 14 ounces each

CHIMICHURRI SAUCE
3 garlic cloves
1 jalapeño chile, chopped
1 large handful fresh Italian parsley
1 large handful fresh cilantro leaves
½ cup white or red wine vinegar
pinch of ground cumin
1⅓ cups extra-virgin olive oil

Compound butters are a great accompaniment to any grilled foods. Very simply, a compound butter is butter that has been flavored with herbs and/or spices and other condiments such as mustard, anchovies, capers and so on. Café de Paris butter has loads of beautiful ingredients flecked through it. When melted over steak it gives the most wonderful flavor and aroma. There is a café in Geneva called Café de Paris that is renowned for its steak with Café de Paris sauce, which is a trade secret but said to contain thyme, chicken livers, Dijon mustard and cream. So this butter is a variation on the theme and, along with French fries and a simple salad, is one of my favorite ways to serve steak.

sirloin steak with café de paris butter

SERVES 4

4 x 8-ounce sirloin steaks
olive oil, for cooking

CAFÉ DE PARIS BUTTER
1 tablespoon ketchup
1 teaspoon Dijon mustard
1 teaspoon small capers, rinsed
2 tablespoons chopped shallots
2 teaspoons finely chopped fresh
   Italian parsley
2 teaspoons chopped fresh chives
1 teaspoon each of chopped fresh
   dill, thyme and oregano leaves
5 fresh tarragon leaves
1 garlic clove, finely chopped
3 anchovy fillets
2 teaspoons Cognac or brandy
2 teaspoons Madeira
1 teaspoon Worcestershire sauce
pinch each of sweet paprika, curry
   powder and cayenne pepper
4 white peppercorns
2 teaspoons sea salt
1 tablespoon lemon juice
finely grated zest of ½ lemon
finely grated zest of ¼ orange
2 cups unsalted butter

To make the café de Paris butter, in a blender, blend the ketchup, mustard, capers, shallots, herbs, garlic, anchovies, Cognac or brandy, Madeira, Worcestershire sauce, spices, salt, lemon juice and citrus zests together. Beat the butter with a whisk until pale and fluffy. Add the blended ingredients, mix well, then roll the mixture in plastic wrap to form a cylinder. Store in the fridge or freezer until needed.

Set up the outdoor grill for direct-heat cooking over high heat. Rub the steaks with oil, season with salt and pepper and bring to room temperature. Grill the steaks for 6–7 minutes on each side, or until done to your liking. Set aside to rest for about 10 minutes, then slice and serve topped with slices of butter.

NOTE: You can freeze the remaining café de Paris butter for up to a month.

My favorite type of meat apart from pork, duck, chicken, beef, kangaroo, quail, rabbit and venison would have to be lamb ... okay okay, I love them all. You can't make a chef choose a favorite meat. That said, though, I do love lamb in all its forms, from the tender rack and tasty rump to the mouthwatering roast leg of lamb and deep-fried brains. This is one of the best ways I have prepared it over the past few years. Ground lamb is a great option to serve at your next grill without having to take out a second mortgage.

spiced lamb skewers with pomegranate molasses

SERVES 4

Soak 8 bamboo skewers in water overnight or use metal skewers.

To make the Turkish spice mix, combine all the ingredients and store in an airtight container until needed.

Combine the lamb with the garlic, tomato, pomegranate molasses and 1 tablespoon of the Turkish spice, mix thoroughly and season with sea salt and cracked black pepper. Form the lamb into 8 small sausage-like shapes around the skewers and refrigerate for 30 minutes to set before cooking.

Combine the yogurt with the pomegranate molasses, mint and sumac.

Set up the outdoor grill for direct-heat cooking over medium heat. Grill the skewers for 3 minutes, then turn and cook for another 3 minutes or until cooked through.

Serve the lamb skewers with the yogurt sauce, pomegranate seeds and mint. Just before serving, drizzle with extra pomegranate molasses.

NOTE: You can keep any remaining Turkish spice mix in an airtight container for up to a month. Look for sumac, a lemony spice, in Middle Eastern markets or specialty food stores.

1 pound ground lamb
1 garlic clove, finely chopped
1 tomato, seeded and finely diced
1 teaspoon pomegranate molasses, plus extra, to serve
seeds of 1 pomegranate, to serve
fresh mint leaves, to serve

TURKISH SPICE MIX
1/3 cup ground cumin
3 tablespoons dried mint
3 tablespoons dried oregano
2 tablespoons sweet paprika
2 tablespoons cracked black pepper
2 teaspoons hot paprika

POMEGRANATE YOGURT
1/2 cup plain yogurt
2 tablespoons pomegranate molasses
1 small handful of fresh mint, chopped
1 teaspoon sumac (see note)

One of the great things about food is how a good meal or even a taste can live in our memories. For me there are certain meals and flavors that I can relive at a moment's notice. Think of a freshly shucked oyster, a beautifully ripe mango, or the first time you tried foie gras. The same can be said for sauces — think brown butter with sage on gnocchi; green peppercorn on a great piece of steak and ketchup on a hamburger. One of my favorite sauces doesn't have a name, it's just a blend of a few ingredients, but when teamed with green tea or soba noodles, it leaves a lasting impression on my tastebuds.

seared scallops with green tea noodles

SERVES 4

16 sea scallops, cleaned
olive oil, for cooking
8 ounces green tea noodles
   or soba noodles
3 tablespoons rice vinegar
2 tablespoons soy sauce
4 tablespoons mirin (Japanese
   cooking wine)
3 tablespoons tahini
1 tablespoon sake
2 tablespoons sesame oil
½ cup olive oil
few drops of chile oil, to taste
3½ ounces silken tofu, cut into
   small cubes
1 tablespoon toasted sesame seeds
   (white and black)
2 tablespoons salmon roe

Season the scallops with sea salt and cracked black pepper and coat lightly in a little olive oil.

Cook the noodles according to the package instructions, then drain and cool under running water, then drain again.

To make the dressing, mix the rice vinegar, soy, mirin, tahini, sake, sesame oil, olive oil and chile oil in a blender or whisk until smooth, then taste. Add more chile oil if you like.

Mix some of the dressing with the noodles to coat, then gently fold in the tofu and sesame seeds.

Place the noodles in serving bowls and spoon some dressing over.

Set up the outdoor grill for direct-heat cooking over high heat. Place a griddle, *plancha* or *piastra* suitable for use on an outdoor grill on the grill to preheat. Cook the scallops on the griddle for 1 minute on each side, or until golden and cooked to your liking, then serve with the noodles and top with the salmon roe.

I used to serve this dish in my Hugos Bondi Beach days. If you want to make things simpler, leave out the fried quail eggs. Marinating the fish overnight starts a curing process but, more importantly, flavors the fish beautifully. The simple yet enticing cucumber salad is good enough to serve on its own. The key is to find a lovely balance of sour, sweet, salty and hot.

rainbow trout fillet with cucumber relish

SERVES 4

Combine the soy and fish sauce in a nonreactive dish. Add the trout and marinate for at least 4 hours and up to 24 hours (the longer the better).

To make the tamarind sauce, fry the chile, garlic and cilantro roots in a little peanut oil in a small saucepan until fragrant, then add the tamarind paste and 2 tablespoons of water. Bring to a simmer for 5 minutes. Add the fish sauce and sugar, strain and blend until smooth.

To make the cucumber relish, combine the vinegar, sugar, ⅔ cup of water and some salt in small saucepan over low heat until the sugar is dissolved. Bring to a boil. Add the cucumbers, shallots, ginger, chile and cilantro. Stir and set aside.

Cook the quail eggs in boiling water (with a splash of vinegar in it) for 2½ minutes. Drain under cold water until cool, then peel and dry. Heat about an inch of peanut oil in a deep saucepan over medium-high heat. Fry the eggs until golden and crisp, then remove with a slotted spoon. Mix the eggs with the fish sauce, chile and cilantro leaves, then cut in half.

Set up the outdoor grill for direct-heat cooking over high heat. Place a griddle, *plancha* or *piastra* suitable for use on an outdoor grill on the grill to preheat. Cook the trout with a touch of peanut oil on the griddle, skin side down, until golden and crisp on one side, then turn over and cook until medium-rare, about 2–3 minutes on each side, or until cooked to your liking.

Drain the cucumber relish and place a small amount on the center of each plate, then top with the trout. Add a little more cucumber relish, drizzle with tamarind sauce and top with the quail eggs. Serve garnished with some salmon roe, if you like.

NOTE: Look for tamarind paste, also called tamarind concentrate, in Latin or Asian markets.

1 cup soy sauce

3 tablespoons Asian fish sauce

4 x 6-ounce rainbow trout fillets, skin on

1 tablespoon peanut oil

1 tablespoon salmon roe (optional)

TAMARIND SAUCE

1 red jalapeño chile, finely chopped

1 garlic clove, finely chopped

2 cilantro roots, chopped

peanut oil, for cooking

1 cup tamarind paste (see note)

2 teaspoons fish sauce

2 teaspoons light brown sugar

CUCUMBER RELISH

6 tablespoons white wine vinegar

6 tablespoons superfine sugar

2 small cucumbers, seeded and sliced

3 shallots, finely sliced

1 tablespoon shredded fresh ginger

1 red serrano chile, thinly sliced

1 handful of fresh cilantro leaves

QUAIL EGGS

6 quail eggs

vinegar, for cooking

peanut oil, for cooking

1 tablespoon Asian fish sauce

1 red serrano chile, finely chopped

1 teaspoon fresh cilantro leaves, finely chopped

I had the pleasure of working with two young New Zealanders, Phil Davenport and Hamish Lindsay, years ago in my kitchen at Hugos Bondi Beach. They are both now executive chefs working for great resorts in Bali. Those early days at Bondi were a very creative time — the boys and I would come into work each day thinking of wonderful new things to do with food ... it was a very special time with such a young crew and no limitations. This is one of those recipes that came together over a beer after work one night, then the next day we tried it and it was fantastic. You can leave out the crabmeat in the rösti if you like.

snapper fillets with potato & crab rösti, spiced spinach & carrot sauce

SERVES 4

4 x 6-ounce snapper fillets

olive oil, for cooking

2 garlic cloves, finely chopped

1 Thai chile, finely chopped

1 tablespoon fresh ginger, finely chopped

7 cups baby spinach leaves

juice of ½ lemon

lemon wedges, to serve

CARROT SAUCE

4 cups carrot juice

4 cardamom pods, lightly toasted and bruised

⅓ cup cold butter, diced

juice of 1 lime

POTATO & CRAB ROSTI

1 large potato, peeled and grated

¼ pound crabmeat

1 egg yolk

1 teaspoon chopped fresh (Italian) parsley

1 tablespoon olive oil

1 tablespoon clarified butter or ghee (see recipe p17)

To make the carrot sauce, reduce the carrot juice and cardamom over a medium heat in a saucepan for 30–40 minutes, or until reduced to ½ cup. Remove from the heat, then whisk in the butter, a piece at a time, until you have a sauce consistency, then strain out the cardamom. Add the lime juice to balance out the richness of the butter and season with salt and pepper.

Set up the outdoor grill for direct-heat cooking over medium-high heat. Place a griddle, *plancha* or *piastra* suitable for use on an outdoor grill on the grill to preheat.

To make the potato and crab rösti, squeeze all the excess moisture out of the grated potato, then mix all the ingredients except the oil and butter. Place about 3 tablespoons of the mixture onto the griddle with the oil. Cook for 3 minutes or until golden. Once the rösti is golden, turn over and top with the clarified butter. Cook the second side until golden. Repeat with remaining mixture.

Meanwhile, rub the fish with some olive oil and salt and pepper. Cook the fish, skin side down, on the griddle for about 3 minutes or until golden, then turn over and cook for another 3 minutes, or until cooked through.

Place the garlic, chile and ginger on the griddle with a touch of olive oil and add the spinach. Cook for 1 minute, then season with salt and pepper and the lemon juice. Drain the cooked spinach.

Pour the carrot sauce in the middle of the serving plates and place the rösti on top. Add the drained spinach, top with the cooked fish and serve with lemon wedges.

I first moved to Sydney from Melbourne more than 15 years ago. It was at the start of my career and I wanted to learn as much as I could. Luckily there were some amazing cooking schools in Sydney and it was at these places that my cooking style started to take shape. I saw how passionate Neil Perry was about Australian produce, David Thompson did a two-hour class on his love affair with a bowl of rice, and I watched Christine Manfield tea-smoke a duck — the flavors were so new and amazing that when I tried the duck I was speechless. So back at Hugos I started playing around with what I could match to the duck and this is the dish I ended up with.

tea-smoked duck breast with foie gras ravioli

SERVES 4

Mix the ingredients for the smoking mixture. Turn on your kitchen ventilation. Line a wok with foil, then place half the smoking mixture on top and turn the heat to medium. Once it starts smoking, place the duck breast, skin side down, in the middle tray of a steamer or on a rack that fits into the wok and cover with a lid. Cook for 7 minutes or until rare, then remove from heat.

To make the orange sauce, place the sugar in a cold saucepan and heat it over medium-low heat until it slowly melts. Add the vinegar and simmer until the sugar is dissolved. Add the orange juice and reduce by half. Add the chicken broth and reduce by half. Add the zest and blend the sauce with the butter and salt and pepper to taste.

To make ravioli, mix foie gras, water chestnuts and pear with a touch of salt. Lay 4 gyoza wrappers on a work surface and brush edges with water. Place a mound of foie gras mixture in the center of each wrapper and place remaining 4 wrappers over mounds. Press down around edges to seal. Cook the ravioli for 1 minute in a saucepan of boiling water. Drain and set aside.

Set up the outdoor grill for direct-heat cooking over medium–high heat. Place a griddle, *plancha* or *piastra* suitable for use on an outdoor grill on the grill to preheat. Cook the duck, skin side down, on the griddle until crispy. Turn over and cook for another minute, then let rest for a few minutes.

Brush the ravioli with a little oil and cook on the griddle until crisp.

Place the spinach onto the griddle and wilt down with some sea salt and pepper, then drain any excess liquid. Heat up orange sauce. Place spinach on serving plates, then top with sliced duck breast and ravioli. Drizzle with tablespoon of orange sauce, top with the fried ginger, if using, and serve.

NOTES: This recipe uses half of the smoking mixture. The remainder will keep for up to 1 month in an airtight container. Foie gras can be found through mail-order sources or high-end butchers. To make the crispy ginger, heat 4 tablespoons vegetable oil in a wok and add 2 teaspoons finely grated ginger. Cook until crispy. Drain on paper towels.

4 x 9-ounce duck breasts
4 ounces foie gras (see note)
1¾ ounces water chestnuts, diced
1¾ ounces pear, diced
8 gyoza or round wonton wrappers
9 cups baby spinach
fried crispy ginger, to serve
  (optional, see note)

ORANGE SAUCE
⅓ cup superfine sugar
3 tablespoons red wine vinegar
2 cups blood orange juice
1 cup chicken broth
finely grated zest of ¼ orange
3½ tablespoons butter, diced

TEA SMOKING MIXTURE
½ cup oolong tea leaves
½ cup jasmine tea leaves
finely grated zest of 3 oranges
4 pieces of dried orange peel
1 cup jasmine rice
1 cup firmly packed light
  brown sugar
5 star anise
1 tablespoon Szechuan peppercorns
6 cinnamon sticks

These next two recipes are just simple dessert ideas. Always make sure though that you clean your grill thoroughly before attempting to grill your fruit as you don't want any residual flavors from your steak marinade or grilled squid to ruin the delicious ripe fruit.

grilled figs with mascarpone & honey

SERVES 4

Whisk together the mascarpone, orange zest, Grand Marnier and cream until thick — do not overwhip or it may split.

Set up the outdoor grill for direct-heat cooking over medium heat. Place a griddle, *plancha* or *piastra* suitable for use on an outdoor grill on the grill to preheat. Place the cut side of the figs into the sugar. Place the figs, skin side down, on the griddle and drizzle with a little honey. Cook for 2–3 minutes until just warm and starting to collapse, then serve with the mascarpone mixture, toasted almonds and another drizzle of honey.

1 cup mascarpone cheese
finely grated zest of 1 orange
2 tablespoons Grand Marnier
1 cup light cream
8 fresh figs, cut into halves
3 tablespoons superfine sugar
4 tablespoons honey
¼ cup almonds, chopped
   and toasted

grilled peaches with amaretto

SERVES 4

2 cups superfine sugar

2 x 2-inch strips orange zest

½ cup fresh orange juice

½ cup amaretto (almond-flavored liqueur, Galliano brand works well)

1 vanilla bean, split lengthwise and seeds scraped

6 firm but ripe peaches, halved and pits removed

½ cup almonds, toasted

ALMOND-AMARETTO CREAM

1¼ cups whipping cream

3 tablespoons confectioners' sugar

1¼ cups mascarpone cheese

2 tablespoons amaretto

4 ounces amaretti cookies, coarsely chopped

To make the almond amaretto cream, beat the cream with 1 tablespoon confectioners' sugar until soft peaks form. Stir the mascarpone with the remaining confectioners' sugar, amaretto and cookies until just combined. Gently fold the whipped cream into the mascarpone mixture until just combined. Refrigerate for at least 4 hours before serving.

Place the sugar, zest, orange juice, amaretto, vanilla seeds and 1 cup of water in a large saucepan. Stir over low heat until the sugar dissolves. Bring to a boil, then remove from the heat and cool until warm. Pour over the peaches in a large baking dish. Set aside to cool.

Set up the outdoor grill for direct-heat cooking over medium-high heat. Place a griddle, *plancha* or *piastra* suitable for use on an outdoor grill on the grill to preheat. Remove the peaches from the syrup, reserving the syrup. Cook the peaches on the oiled griddle for 5 minutes or until golden brown.

Place the peaches on a platter and pour some of the syrup over the top. Garnish with the toasted almonds and serve with the almond amaretto cream on the side.

Essentially with this cocktail, you can throw any fruit in a blender but we have spruced it up a bit by adding kaffir (makrut) lime leaf to its foundation and complementing it with the elderflower liqueur.

floral delight cocktail

SERVES 4–6

Add the watermelon and kaffir lime to a pitcher and muddle. Add the lemon juice, liqueur and apple juice with some ice, stir well, pour into glasses and top with soda.

GLASS: Highball
GARNISH: Kaffir lime leaf

12 large chunks watermelon
8 kaffir (makrut) lime leaves
2 ounces lemon juice
1 ounce elderflower liqueur
4 ounces apple juice
2 ounces club soda

The breakfast martini was created by Salvatore Calabrese in London. It is a wonderfully simple drink using everyday ingredients. With a little twist, you can create your own signature variation — try using a little raspberry jam instead of marmalade.

breakfast martini

SERVES 4

6 ounces gin
2 ounces Cointreau
4 ounces lemon juice
½ ounce citrus syrup
8 teaspoons marmalade

Add a quarter of all the ingredients into a cocktail shaker, add some ice, shake and strain into a chilled glass. Repeat with the remaining ingredients.

GLASS: Martini glass
GARNISH: Orange twist

How you serve Pimm's is up to you, as long as there is lots of fruit, some mint and a sliver of cucumber in there somewhere. You can also warm the Pimm's with apple juice for when the weather gets cooler.

pimm's cup

SERVES 4–6

8 ounces Pimm's No. 1 Cup
4 ounces lemon juice
2½ ounces sugar syrup
1 cucumber, sliced
1 orange, sliced
¼ cantaloupe, chopped
4–6 fresh mint sprigs
¼ cup grapes
2 cups club soda

Add all the ingredients to a carafe with some ice and stir well. Serve in glasses.

GLASS: Highball glass
GARNISH: Orange slice, cucumber slice and mint sprig

A sgropino is traditionally made with sherbet, lemon liqueur and prosecco, an Italian sparkling wine; however this is a real treat with some green apple sherbet and a hint of apple liqueur. You can even try mango sherbet with a touch of mint and finished with prosecco.

apple sgropino

SERVES 4–6

Add all the ingredients except for the prosecco to a blender, then blend and pour into glasses. Top each glass with prosecco, stir through and serve.

GLASS: Champagne flute
GARNISH: Candied apple
NOTE: Cut the apple into very thin slices and press into some superfine sugar. Cook in the oven on a low heat (235°F) until crisp.

⅓ cup gin
1¼ ounces apple liqueur
½ ounce lime juice
½ ounce sugar syrup
  (see recipe p84)
4 large scoops apple sherbet
8 ounces prosecco (Italian
  sparkling wine)
candied apple, to garnish (see note)

The original daiquiri stems from 1896 and was made with white rum, lime and sugar syrup. The Campari in this version adds a bitter element and with the passionfruit you pick up some natural sweetness to balance it out.

dry daiquiri

SERVES 4–6

Add a quarter or a sixth of the ingredients to a cocktail shaker. Add ice, shake and strain into a chilled glass. Repeat with the remaining ingredients.

GLASS: Martini glass
GARNISH: Large teaspoon of passion fruit pulp.
NOTE: Frozen passion fruit pulp can be found in Latin markets. Thaw before using.

7 ounces white rum
2½ ounces lime juice
1¼ ounces sugar syrup
  (see recipe p84)
½ ounce Campari
8 teaspoons of passion fruit
  pulp (see note)

index

weldon**owen**

415 Jackson Street, Suite 200, San Francisco, CA 94111
Telephone: 415 291 0100 Fax: 415 291 8841
www.wopublishing.com

Weldon Owen is a division of
BONNIER

First published in the United States in 2011

First published in 2009 by
Murdoch Books Australia
Pier 8/9, 23 Hickson Road
Millers Point NSW 2000
www.murdochbooks.com.au

Editor: Daniela Bertollo
Designer: Reuben Crossman
Photographer: Anson Smart
Stylist: David Morgan
Food editor: Sonia Greig

Color separations by Splitting Image Colour Studio,
Melbourne, Australia.
Printed by 1010 Printing International Limited in 2010.
PRINTED IN CHINA.

10 9 8 7 6 5 4 3 2 1

Library of Congress Control Number: 2010941193

ISBN: 978-1-61628-116-8